Sophocles

Twayne's World Authors Series

Greek Literature

TWAS 731

SOPHOCLES
Cologne Philosopher Mosaic, third century A.D.
Photograph courtesy of the
Römisch-Germanisches Museum der Stadt Köln

Sophocles

By Ruth Scodel

Harvard University

Twayne Publishers • Boston

Sophocles

Ruth Scodel

Copyright © 1984 by G. K. Hall & Company
All Rights Reserved
Published by Twayne Publishers
A Division of G. K. Hall & Company
70 Lincoln Street
Boston, Massachusetts 02111

Book Production by Marne B. Sultz

Book Design by Barbara Anderson

Printed on permanent/durable acid-free
paper and bound in the United States of
America.

**Library of Congress Cataloging in
Publication Data**

Scodel, Ruth.
  Sophocles.

  (Twayne's world authors series; TWAS 731. Greek
literature)
  Bibliography: p. 146
  Includes index.
  1. Sophocles—Criticism and interpretation.   I. Title.
II. Series: Twayne's world authors series ; TWAS 731.
III. Series: Twayne's world authors series. Greek
literature.
PA4417.S44 1984   882'.01   83–26563
ISBN 0–8057–6578–6

In memory of
Cedric H. Whitman
and for Anne

Contents

About the Author

Ruth Scodel received her Ph.D. from Harvard University in 1978, and is now associate professor of the classics at Harvard. She is the author of *The Trojan Trilogy of Euripides* (1980), and of articles and notes on Greek poetry in learned journals.

Preface

Sophocles is firmly established among the greatest authors of the Western tradition, and his work is the subject of a vast secondary literature. This exalted place, however, does not make him easy for the general reader. He composed in a language which very few people now study, and in a culture which, although it is in so many ways the direct ancestor of our own, is in some respects profoundly different. His great central characters and their dilemmas can still speak directly to us; Oedipus, Antigone, and Electra need no critical help to move a reader or an audience. But the sophistication, subtlety, and difficulty of his work are not so immediately accessible, and much of the secondary literature is either directed at specialists or concerned with particular aspects of Sophocles' art. This book has two goals. First, I have tried to offer general readers an idea of the background of Sophocles' works, especially their literary predecessors—Homer, the Epic Cycle, and Aeschylus—and certain aspects of Greek religion. Second, I have discussed issues of interpretation, with emphasis on the vision of the world which emerges from the Sophoclean plays. This is not an attempt to extract a "message" or a philosophy from the plays, but to examine the issues the dramas raise and how meaning arises from what the characters say, do, and suffer. I have tried to mention, at least, a wide range of issues and kinds of interpretation, but I have given special attention to the relationship between gods and human beings in Sophocles. Much of the action in Sophocles is performed by gods and mortals together. This aspect of Sophoclean drama is especially difficult for modern readers to appreciate, but it contributes a great deal to the richness and ambiguity of the plays.

Inevitably, certain areas have been neglected. For example, the lyric qualities of Sophocles' work are so hard to convey in translation that Sophocles as a lyric poet has been largely ignored. While I have tried to indicate where I have taken controversial positions (and have sometimes doubtless slipped into polemic), some points have had to be passed over lightly. I have given rather less attention than I would have liked to strictly dramaturgical matters, because they often raise very technical problems of production. One tendency is deliberate: I have analyzed each drama as a web of actions and relations to which all the characters are subordinate, and I have placed less emphasis on the protagonists than most Sophoclean criticism of the last thirty years, although I hope I have not slighted the brilliant, lonely central figures. This placement of emphasis is in part an attempt to correct what seems to me an excess in earlier criticism, and in part an avoidance of one aspect which has received excellent treatment (the interested reader should consult the books of K. Reinhardt, C. H. Whitman, and B. M. W. Knox listed in the bibliography). The positive side of my method is its attention to what makes Sophocles endlessly puzzling: his way of presenting conflicting explanations without directing us how to choose among them; his love of irony and ambiguity; his fascination with illusion and deceit; his habit of stressing yet negating time.

The translations in this book are my own, and are purely utilitarian. A reader using the translations of Sir Richard Jebb will notice my frequent indebtedness. My thanks are due to Harvard University for the semester's leave during which I accomplished much of the actual writing. Professor Peter Burian, who read the manuscript for Twayne, made many helpful suggestions. For advice and encouragement I am grateful to many students and colleagues, especially Professor James Halporn of Indiana University, and at Harvard Professors Zeph Stewart, Albert Henrichs, Richard Thomas, and Jeffrey Rusten. The manuscript was delivered to the publisher in the summer of 1982 and work published since then could not be taken into account.

Ruth Scodel

Harvard University

Editions and Abbreviations

Sophocles: R. C. Jebb. *Sophocles: The Plays and Fragments.* Cambridge: Cambridge University Press. Individual plays, 1883–96; reprinted, 1902–8; text without translation and commentary reprinted 1897; full reprint, Amsterdam: Hakkert, 1966.

Fragments: S. Radt. *Tragicorum Graecorum Fragmenta IV: Sophocles.* Göttingen: Vanderhoeck und Ruprecht, 1980 (Radt).

Editions of Other Authors

Aeschylus: H. J. Mette. *Die Fragmente der Tragödien des Aischylos.* Berlin: Akademie-Verlag, 1959 (Mette). English translation in: H. W. Smyth. *Aeschylus ii.* Cambridge, Mass.: Loeb Classical Library, 1926. Reprint 1957 with a supplement by H. Lloyd-Jones (Smyth).

Bacchylides: B. Snell and H. Maehler. *Bacchylidis Carmina cum Fragmentis.* Leipzig: Teubner, 1970 (Snell-Maehler).

Elegiac and Iambic Poets: M. L. West. *Iambi et Elegi Graeci.* Oxford: Oxford University Press, 1972 (West).

Epic Cycle: T. W. Allen, *Homeri Opera V.* Oxford: Oxford University Press, 1912 (Allen). English translation: H. G. Evelyn-White. *Hesoid, Homeric Hymns, and Homerica.* Cambridge, Mass.: Loeb Classical Library, 1914 (Evelyn-White).

Hesoid: R. Merkelbach and M. L. West, *Fragmenta Hesiodea.* Oxford: Oxford University Press, 1967 (Merkelbach-West).

Lyric Poetry: D. Page. *Poetae Melici Graeci.* Oxford: Oxford University Press, 1962 (PMG).

Pindar: B. Snell and H. Maehler, *Pindari Carmina cum Fragmentis.* 2 vols. Leipzig: Teubner, 1971–75. (Snell-Maehler). Vol. 1: Epinicians; Vol. 2: Fragments.

Chronology

Chapter One
Sophocles and Athens

The Fifth Century

The name of Sophocles is indelibly associated with Athens at the height of her glory. Like the sculptures of the Parthenon, his plays are symbols of Athenian greatness. This symbolic quality is at least partly justified. Sophocles' career coincided closely with the height of Athenian power, and he was active in his city's service. His work as a poet is central within the flowering of thought and literature whose focus was Athens. At least a brief outline of the busy history of Athens in the fifth century B.C. is thus important for any study of the tragedian.[1]

When Sophocles was born, around 496, Athens, though not a backwater, was neither an intellectual center nor a great power within the Greek world. She was one among the Greek city-states of the Greek mainland and islands, the coasts of Asia Minor and the Black Sea, southern Italy and Sicily. On the mainland, Sparta was more powerful by far, and all the little states of the Aegean were dwarfed by the Persian Empire to the east. But Athens's cultural life had been fostered by the tyrant Pisistratus and his sons, and in 508–6 a democracy had been established in the midst of inner turmoil and Spartan intervention. Athens and its countryside, Attica, was organized by local wards, the demes, each joined with demes in other parts of Attica so that ten tribes were formed, none with a regional base. The chief magistrates, the archons, were elected from the two highest of four property classes, and after their year in office became members of the Council of the Areopagus. A second council (Boule), the Council of Five Hundred, was chosen by lot from an elected pool, and prepared business for the assembly of all adult male citizens.

This newly democratic Athens had its first great triumph in 490. Eight years before, Athens and Eretria, on the nearby island of Euboea, had sent help to the Ionian Greek cities who were in revolt against the rule of Persia. Now the Persian Empire sought to avenge itself in a punitive expedition. Eretria was sacked, and the Persians invaded Attic territory on the coast, at Marathon. The Athenians sought help from Sparta; but the Spartans came too late, and the Athenians won a complete victory on their own. The victory greatly boosted Athenian self-confidence and prestige. Around 487 the election of archons was changed, so that they were chosen by lot from an elected pool, like the Council; this change naturally weakened both the archonship itself and the Areopagus, the most aristocratic institutions. The people were beginning to feel their strength. From now on the most powerful office in Athens was the generalship; a board of ten, one from each tribe, was elected annually.

In 483 a great find of silver was made at Laurium in Attica, and the brilliant Themistocles, who envisioned Athens as a seapower, persuaded the people not to distribute the money among the citizens, but to build a new fleet. In 480 the new warships proved themselves, for the Persians returned under the personal command of King Xerxes. This was no mere punitive strike: the aim was the conquest of Greece. The great Persian army, both land and sea forces, invaded from the north, and the first attempts of the allied Greeks to stop them failed. The Athenians abandoned their city and moved their dependents to the island of Salamis; the city and its temples were ravaged by the invaders. But Themistocles lured the Persian fleet into offering battle in the narrow strait between Salamis and the mainland, where greater numbers were less of an advantage, and the Greeks, with the Athenians the backbone of the fleet, won a spectacular victory. The Persians retreated. Though they invaded again the following year, they were again defeated, this time on land at Plataea, while a Greek force was again victorious at Mycale on the coast of Asia Minor, freeing the Greek cities there. But Sparta was not eager to pursue such overseas operations; Athens was. In 478/7 a large number of Asiatic and island cities formed the Delian League under Athenian leadership as a perpetual alliance against the Persians. Larger cities were to contribute ships to the allied fleet, smaller ones money. The treasurers, Hellenotamiae, were Athenian officials.

This league was the basis of the Athenian Empire. Gradually fewer and fewer states provided ships, and with the tribute Athens developed her own navy. Rebellious allies were reduced to subjection to Athens. At the same time, when the power of the city rested in the common sailors, the power of the common people could not be withstood. In 462 the Areopagus was stripped of all its powers except that of trying homicide cases. In 457/6 the archonship was opened to the third property class. And at some time in this period came the most famous innovation of Athenian democracy: pay for public offices and for the jurymen on the very large panels which tried the endless flood of new litigation. Thus it became possible for the poor to participate in government not only in law, but in fact. Through the middle years of the fifth century the leader in both imperial policy and domestic reform was Pericles.

This close contemporary of Sophocles (born around 495) was a remarkable leader: personally austere, he succeeded in dominating the people rather than being dominated by them, so that Thucydides says (2.65.9) that his government was "in name a democracy, but in fact the rule of the first man." He was associated with the philosopher Anaxagoras and the sculptor Phidias. In 447 he served as building commissioner for the new temple of Athena Polias, the Parthenon; the allied tribute paid for the glorification of Athens through the temples whose ruins now adorn the Acropolis.

The growth of Athenian power naturally alarmed Sparta, head of the Peloponnesian League of mainland states. When war began in 431, Pericles was confident: while Sparta could invade and ravage Attica, the citizens could retreat into the fortified city and conduct operations by sea. But in 430, plague broke out in the overcrowded city. Morale temporarily collapsed. Pericles was removed from office and fined, then restored; he died in 429, and his successors lacked his restraint. Demagoguery came into flower. In 425 Athens achieved a brilliant success at Pylos, and Sparta sued for peace, but Athens refused. In 424 Athens met with severe losses, and a year's truce followed; in 422 peace became possible when both Sparta's most brilliant general, Brasidas, and the chief popular leader at Athens, Cleon, were killed. Even this peace was no real peace; not all Sparta's allies accepted it, and anti-Spartan intrigue continued. In 416 Athens committed the most notorious atrocity of the period, attacking the neutral island of Melos, and, when the island refused submission, killing its male population and enslaving the women. In the following year the Athenians, asked for help by Segesta in Sicily, conceived the grand scheme of conquering the island, and sent a large and badly mismanaged expedition. In 413 the force was utterly destroyed; the loss was catastrophic.

Meanwhile Sparta recommenced operations in Attica, and with the help of subsidies from the Persians built a fleet. The enemies of democracy had their chance; after the disaster special commissioners were appointed. Athens held on through 412, using a reserve fund established by Pericles to rebuild, but in 411 the coup took place. Many of the lower classes were away with the fleet on Samos; a double revolution was planned for both Athens and Samos. The oligarchs held a campaign of intimidation. There were two main groups: one favored a government of all those rich enough to serve in the infantry, the other sought control for itself, a small band of conspirators. The moderates were bribed with the promise of a change in Persian policy and help for Athens. A Council of Four Hundred, the oligarchs and their supporters, was formed, but it was soon overthrown when it failed to meet its promises. The moderate government which followed lasted less than a year, for new successes by the fleet revived the strength of the popular party. Athens, weary as she was, continued to fight, and even rejected an offer of peace after the Athenian victory in the naval battle of Arginusae in 406. But the following year the fleet was surprised at Aegospotami on the Hellespont, and Athens was blockaded. Sophocles was fortunate: he died in 406 or the following year, and did not see the final surrender of Athens in 404.

The Dramatic Festival

The earliest origins of tragedy are controversial and obscure, but fortunately of little relevance for Sophocles. By the time he came to know tragedy, it was a highly developed, though still young art. Tragedy formed a part of the celebration of the Great or City Dionysia, a festival organized by the tyrant Pisistratus, in the spring month of Elaphebolion (usually in March).[2] Tragedy was thus created in a public and sacred context. This element should not be exaggerated, however. It is difficult for a native of modern, secular society to imagine how permeated was ancient Greek life by religion, and equally difficult for an heir of the Judeo-Christian tradition to sense the complex nature of archaic and classical religion. Separation of church and state was unimaginable, for the welfare of the city depended on the goodwill of the gods; at the same time a glorification of the city's gods could also be a glorification of the city itself. Piety and patriotism were often united. Further, the center of Greek religion was in cult, not faith; a matter of daily practice, not dogma or sacred books. Practically all slaughter of domestic animals was sacrificial, so that any feast was a sacred occasion, while sacred occasions were welcome chances for a feast. Pericles in the Funeral Oration put in his mouth by Thucydides (2.38) calls the Athenian festivals and competitions "relaxations for the mind" and praises Athens for celebrating more of them than other cities. A less secular mind would have called them also the proof of Attic piety, but holy day and holiday cannot fully be distinguished.

The basis of tragedy is the union of two kinds of poetry. Spoken verse belongs chiefly to actors, sung verse to the chorus. The basic pattern of a drama is that a scene spoken by actors ends with an exit, and a song divides the episode from the next, which is opened by an actor's entrance.[3] This pattern, however, is open to much variation. The chorus enters the orchestra—its "dancing space"— early in the play, and rarely exits before the end. A chorus has a composite personality; when a chorus participates in a spoken exchange, the chorus-leader speaks on its behalf. In the tragedy Sophocles knew as a child, there were only two actors, who wore lifelike masks. By changing mask and costume an actor could play different characters, while a character without a speaking part in a given scene could be played by an extra. Extras also accompanied royal characters as attendants. The early tragic stage was simply an open place for dancing, but the Sophoclean tragedies were performed before a stage-building with a central door, representing the tent of Ajax or the cave of Philoctetes. The subject matter was heroic legend or, occasionally, contemporary history. Tragedy was governed by a stylistic decorum which provided great events with a grand style, but only real vulgarity was absolutely excluded, and language could range from the almost colloquial to the grandiose. Tragedy was performed before a huge audience (perhaps fifteen thousand) in the open air; it was expected to treat major issues, religious, ethical, and in the widest sense political.

Tragedies were performed in competition. The archon in charge of the festival "granted a chorus" to the three tragedians he chose from those who applied; these received state-paid actors, while the expense of the chorus was carried by wealthy citizens as a kind of income tax. This man, the *choregus*, could increase his prestige by being lavish. The poet produced his own play; each produced three tragedies and an afterpiece called a satyr-play from its chorus of beast-men. Each poet's production was on a separate day, starting early in the morning; this made possible the Aeschylean tetralogy, three tragedies telling one story and the satyr-play a lighthearted version of the same theme.

Unfortunately, we have no play of Aeschylus early enough to represent the tragedy Sophocles first knew, nor is any surviving play of Sophocles early enough to show obvious Aeschylean influence. Sophocles is credited in the tradition[4] with introducing the third actor, which first appears in Aeschylus's *Oresteia* of 458; if this is true, Sophocles must have had considerable influence even as a young poet. The same source credits him with inventing "scene-painting": while nothing approaching a realistic set was ever used, the erection of a permanent stage-building as a backdrop may have inspired more scenic elaboration. These hints at development are important less for themselves than because they show how the rules of tragedy were not inflexible.

Sophocles' Life

Sources for the life of Sophocles are anecdotal and unreliable.[5] The surviving ancient biography is a curious mixture of inferences from the poetry itself, naive belief in jokes from comedies, folklore, and genuine information. For Sophocles few dates of production are given, unfortunately, so that his artistic career cannot be traced in detail, but we do have at least some idea of his public life.

While the sources differ as to the date of his birth, the 496 of the Parian Marble (a chronological inscription listing events down to 264 B.C.) or 495/4 of the biography would be appropriate. His deme was Colonus, just outside Athens, and although deme membership was hereditary and thus not proof of origin, this was probably his native place. His family was certainly wealthy, and he is said to have studied music with a famous teacher, Lamprus. His first victory came in 468 with a tetralogy including the *Triptolemus;* Triptolemus was a hero associated with the Eleusinian mysteries, and the play's theme may have struck a note of patriotic piety. *Ajax* and *Women of Trachis* may have been written in the fifties or forties.

In the year 443/2 Sophocles enters history: a Sophocles of Colonus, (almost certainly the poet), is listed on the inscribed tribute lists as a Hellenotamias. This was a major state office, requiring financial responsibility (probably restricted to the highest property class), but not usually a political stepping-stone.[6] That Sophocles held it shows both the respect in which he was held and his dedication: though most of the minute work was doubtless performed by the clerk, the task of the treasurer must have been time-consuming. His holding the post also suggests that he supported Athenian imperial policy. In 441/40, Sophocles served as general in the war against Samos, which had rebelled. According to the ancient prefatory note to *Antigone,* he was elected because of popular admiration of this play. The story may not be true, but the dates of plays were known (Aristotle had collected them in his *Didascaliae*), so that at least the chronology may be right; we know, however, that Euripides was victorious in 441. *Antigone* is therefore tentatively dated to 442, although Sophocles would have had a busy time of it. The story is not impossible. At the time of the elections, the Athenians would not have expected the Samians to revolt, and might have chosen to honor the poet in this way; but Sophocles seems in general to have been a very popular man.

As general, he sailed to collect a squadron from Lesbos, and was entertained by the Athenian "honorary consul" on Chios. Some anecdotes of this visit were recorded by Ion of Chios, a contemporary poet, in his *Visits,* and for once, at least, the gossip is believable and comes from a source close to the subject: Ion describes some literary joking about a handsome serving boy, and Sophocles' success in obtaining a kiss—he claimed, according to Ion, to be a better "strategist" than Pericles thought. Ion remarks that Sophocles said and did much that was witty while drinking, "but in politics he was no cleverer nor more efficient than any upper-class Athenian." All this rings true—the tone of friendly banter is in place, and the charm is mentioned in the biography and accords well with the epitaph he is given in Aristophanes' *Frogs,* where in the year after his death he is called *eukolos:* easygoing or good-natured (line 82).

In 421 Aristophanes' *Peace* (697 ff.) shows another, obscure side. He is said to have "become Simonides"—a poet famed for avarice—and it is said that "being old and rotten, for profit he would sail on wicker-work." The line parodies a proverb Sophocles used in a drama, but its meaning is far from clear. In the following year the cult of Asclepius was brought to Athens, and Sophocles entertained the god, in the form of his sacred snake, while his shrine was built; the poet was already, apparently, the priest of an obscure healing hero associated with Asclepius, Halon. He also composed a paean to Asclepius. As a reward for his service he was given a cult of his own under the name of Dexion, the Receiver.[7] In 412 he was one of the special commissioners, *probouloi;* Aristotle[8] mentions an occasion when, challenged by the oligarch Pisander as to whether he had not voted for the establishment of the Four Hundred, he replied that he had, "for there was nothing better to be done." It may not be a coincidence that his only firmly dated play, *Philoctetes* of 409, depicts the political world as deeply corrupt.

Though stories of his quarreling with his sons are likely to be fiction, his two marriages need not be doubted; his son Iophon had his first tragic victory in 435, while from another marriage he had a son, Ariston, whose son the younger Sophocles was also a tragedian. Of Sophocles' old age we have a near-contemporary anecdote in Plato's *Republic* (329B–C): asked by someone whether he was still capable of intercourse with a woman, Sophocles replied, "Speak no ill-omened word! I have escaped from it with joy, as if I'd run away from an insane and wild master."

After his death in 406, the comic poets call him lucky. Aristophanes' *Frogs* praises his good nature, and Phrynichus (T. 105 Radt) speaks of his happiness in writing so many fine tragedies and dying before he endured any evil (a reference to the fall of Athens). His genius did not fail him to the end, for his last surviving work, *Oedipus at Colonus,* was produced only posthumously.

What emerges from the biography is a coherent picture of a highly urbane man, and a meticulous artist. According to the Byzantine encyclopedia *Suda* he composed a prose work *On the Chorus;* whether or not this is true, the conversation recorded by Ion shows his self-consciousness in art, and we are told that he increased the number of chorus members from twelve to fifteen. He won eighteen victories at the Dionysia, and probably others at a lesser festival, the Lenaea, where tragic competitions were held from about 440 on. The ancient scholars of Alexandria knew 130 plays, but considered seven of these spurious. We are told that he was never third in the competition. Both his piety and his public service was conspicuous, but this does not prove that he was serenely faithful in religious belief or simple in his contemplation of life.

Intellectual Currents

During Sophocles' lifetime, an intellectual revolution took place. At its center were the Sophists, professional teachers of success in public life, but other intellectuals also participated.[9] Inherited wisdom was challenged in almost every area; the common elements in every field are rationalism and relativism. Success demanded rhetoric, and sophistic rhetorical training involved the ability to argue both sides of any question, arguments from probability in preference to reliance on facts, and self-conscious attention to language. A sophistically trained speaker could "make the worse argument the better": the technique revealed the ambiguity of the relation between language and truth.

The distinction between *physis* ("nature") and *nomos* ("custom") was essential to much fifth-century debate. A growing ethnographical literature—represented for us by the work of Sophocles' friend Herodotus—showed how different were different human societies. But if customs varied so widely, local custom lost its simple authority. Furthermore, sophistic theorizing argued that instead of having degenerated from the Golden Age of mythology, humanity had begun in a condition of savagery, and had progressed through technical advances and the development of social life. The antithesis between nature and custom was explored in many directions: political theory, based on ideas of government as a social contract or agreement among men, and on comparison among different forms of government, was developed; on the darker side, the antithesis was exploited by those who were hungry for power to dismiss the claims of justice as "merely" conventional. All kinds of social distinctions were opened to question, once nature and convention were separated: the upper-class Greek's superiority to the lower classes, slaves, women, and foreigners could be doubted and debated.

Natural philosophers were also active; the philosopher Anaxagoras, a friend of Pericles, gave the true cause of eclipses and used a famous meteorite fall to support his argument that the heavenly bodies were stones heated by friction. Such theorizing seemed to many people to undermine religion, and the Sophists contributed to overturning traditional belief by including the origins of belief in gods in the history of human culture. Nothing was immune to discussion or accepted without question. The most famous statement of the period is the Sophist Protagoras's "Man is the measure of all things—of how those that exist exist, and how those that do not exist do not exist." This is not a vague humanistic boast, but the declaration of a subjective philosophy in which reality depends on individual perceptions. If I feel cold, but you feel warm, it is both

warm and cold. While the details of Protagoras's views are difficult
to reconstruct, to ordinary people he must have seemed to be dis-
solving the stable world into a meaningless riot of perceptions and
opinions.

The *Clouds* of Aristophanes (ca. 417), a satire of Socrates, shows
how intellectual life appeared to the popular mind. Some of the
jokes are at the expense of the countryman who comes to Socrates
for help in escaping his debts: he has never seen a map, and thinks
Sparta should be moved farther away. The Socrates of the play, in
accordance with a theory identifying the substance of mind with
air, hangs in a basket so as to think better. He gives explanations
of weather which ignore the gods, and has replaced Zeus (whose
name in the gentive case is "Dios") with the Vortex ("Dinos"). His
teaching includes metrics and grammatical problems. He can make
the worse argument the better, and the Unjust Argument, who
inhabits his school, urges the student to "follow nature" by com-
mitting adultery. When the countryman's son has been trained in
Socrates' school, he beats his father and defends the practice by
analogy with roosters.

Athens was at the center of the new thought. At the age of fifty-
five Sophocles composed an ode to the historian Herodotus (fr. 5
West), who around this time joined the colony of Thurii, founded
under Pericles' inspiration in 443 and given its law-code by Protagoras. Sophocles several times shows his familiarity with Herodotus's work; for example, in *Oedipus at Colonus* (337–41) Oedipus
says that his sons follow Egyptian customs. Another poem (fr. 1
West) begins with a joke about the difficulty in putting the name
of the philosopher Archelaus into verse; Archelaus was a follower
of Anaxagoras who concerned himself with issues of *nomos* and *physis*.
There is no doubt that Sophocles knew the thought of his day. His
plays, however, unlike those of his younger contemporary Euripides,
do not often refer explicitly to currently debated topics. The "Ode
on Man" of *Antigone* (332–75) gives a sophistic account of human
progress; in *Philoctetes* the protagonist's life on a desert island is
modeled on that of primitive man. In *Oedipus the King* (583–602)
Creon uses arguments from probability to prove that he would not
have wanted to overthrow Oedipus. The speech helps characterize
Creon as a cautious and reasonable man, lacking the grandeur of
Sophocles' main characters.* In *Antigone,* when the heroine argues
that "unwritten ordinances" from Zeus commanded her to bury her

brother (450–70), the speech may arise from a current debate on whether universal, unwritten laws govern humanity in addition to local codes, but the speech is not primarily an entry in this debate, but an affirmation of Antigone's belief that the gods require her deed. In *Ajax,* Menelaus sneers at Teucer as an archer instead of a hoplite, who fought at close quarters (1120), while Agamemnon calls him a bastard of a non-Greek mother (1228–34). Euripides would have had the characters debate whether these judgments had a real basis or were foolish conventions; Sophocles uses them to characterize his actors but does not explore them in general terms. The Sophoclean drama, with its intense concentration on individuals and their actions, was not suited to generalizing argument.

In *Oedipus the King,* Oedipus's intellectual self-confidence reflects the spirit of the sophistic age. The world of the drama, however, is not the comprehensible and lucid order imagined by philosophers; neither is it the chaos of the Euripidean stage, where traditional certainties have been abolished and nothing has replaced them. The characters of Sophocles live in a traditional order, in which the authority of the gods is unquestioned and the characters live by inherited aristocratic values. But this order is presented at its most complex and problematic. While *Oedipus the King* rejects the tendency to treat all problems as rationally soluble, it offers no banal alternatives. Instead of looking at traditional belief from the outside, Sophocles presents tragic situations which test it on its own terms. Although the intellectual crisis of the fifth century only occasionally appears openly on the Sophoclean stage, the challenge it offered to the inherited view of the universe and humanity's place in it added intensity to his portrayal of the difficulties and mysteries that view implied.

Chapter Two

Against Time
and Chance: *Ajax*

The Myth and the Character

Ajax was a great hero of the Trojan War, second only to Achilles, according to Homer's *Iliad* (2. 768–69). When Achilles was slain, his armor was offered as a prize for the best of the other Greeks; but it was awarded to the crafty Odysseus instead of Ajax. Ajax killed himself. This is the simplest form of the myth behind Sophocles' drama, as the story appears, for example, in the *Odyssey,* where Odysseus, visiting the Underworld, sees the shade of Ajax, and speaks apologetically of the Judgment as an expression of divine hostility to the Greeks. Ajax, however, refuses to answer (11. 540–65).

There were different versions of how the arms were awarded and how Ajax met his death. The *Odyssey* mentions "the children of the Trojans and Pallas Athena" (11. 547): in one of the post-Homeric epics known collectively as the *Epic Cycle,* spies overheard two Trojan girls comparing Ajax and Odysseus; one praised Ajax for rescuing the body of Achilles, but the other, inspired by Athena, said that "even a woman could carry a burden."[1] For the older contemporary of Sophocles, the lyric poet Pindar, Ajax, who lost in a secret ballot of the Greeks through being no rhetorician, exemplifies the destructive power of envy and ignorance.[2] While both Homer and Pindar mention only the suicide, the *Cycle* included the story of how Ajax went mad in his grief over the loss of the arms and slaughtered the cattle the Greek army had gathered as booty. Unfortunately, Aeschylus's treatment of the theme in his trilogy about Ajax is not known.[3]

Outside the story of his death, however, we have a clear picture of Ajax in the Homeric poems. He is the great hero of defense, characterized by his huge shield, and he is the only major hero who is never directly helped by a god. In *Iliad* 7 he fights a formal duel with the Trojan leader, Hector, and when night parts them (Ajax having the advantage) they exchange gifts, Ajax giving a shield-strap and Hector a sword. In the ninth book, Ajax is the third member of an embassy sent to persuade Achilles, who has withdrawn from battle because he is angry at King Agamemnon, to return. Odysseus lists the gifts Agamemnon offers, and is rebuffed. Old Phoenix, Achilles' tutor, invokes honor, and is told not to serve Agamemnon. Ajax speaks briefly and from the heart. Achilles is cruel to reject his friends; and to Ajax Achilles answers that the speech is after his own heart, though anger prevents him from yielding. There is an affinity between these two, which Sophocles will exploit. But Ajax is always the defender of the values of loyalty and friendship in the poems, constantly encouraging his comrades as he fights alongside his illegitimate brother, the archer Teucer. He also delivers one of the most moving prayers in Greek literature.[4] Supernatural darkness covers the battlefield, so that Ajax, defending the body of dead Patroclus, cannot find anyone to deliver a message to Achilles, and cries: "Father Zeus, save the sons of the Achaeans from this cloud / And make clear air; permit us to see. Kill us in the light, if that is your will."

The Plot

The play begins at daybreak, with the goddess Athena greeting Odysseus outside Ajax's tent. Odysseus is tracking the killer of the Greek cattle, and Athena confirms that this is indeed Ajax. In his anger over the Judgment, Ajax set out by night to murder Odysseus and the leaders of the army, Agamemnon and Menelaus. Athena, however, drove him mad, so that he attacked the cattle. She calls Ajax out, after making Odysseus invisible. He congratulates her on her help, and he glories in his success. At present he is torturing Odysseus before killing him; Athena objects to this, but he insists. The goddess points the moral of the display. No one was more foresighted than Ajax or better at acting appropriately, but the power of the gods has reduced him to this. She warns the pity-filled Odysseus not to be boastful toward the gods or proud because of strength or wealth, for a single day can change everything for mortals: "The gods love the self-restrained, and hate the bad" (133).

Man and divinity exit, and the chorus enters. These are followers of Ajax from his native island of Salamis (politically part of Attica).

They are confused by what they have heard, and hope that Ajax will come forth to dispel their fears. But Tecmessa, the concubine of Ajax, emerges instead (200). She describes the events of the previous night and morning: his night exit, his return with the cattle, his conversation with nothing at the door, and his recovery of reason, which has plunged him into deepest grief. Cries come from within, and the doors open to reveal Ajax among the cattle (346).[5] He laments his humiliation and sees the hand of Athena. In a long speech he deliberates: his name (which resembles the Greek "alas") has proven true. Achilles would have awarded him the arms. Hated by both gods and army, he must find a way to die honorably without helping his enemies. Tecmessa tries to calm him, citing her own endurance of fortune (she is a captured princess) and the evil that will befall her if Ajax dies. He is unmoved, and sends for his son. He envies the child's innocence. But the true son of Ajax will not fear the blood of the cattle. Ajax prays that his son will be luckier than he, but otherwise like him. He goes inside, refusing to soften (595).

The chorus sings of longing for Salamis and the coming grief of Ajax's parents. But Ajax emerges, and speaks of the power of time (646–92). Natural forces yield to each other, and he too feels pity. In a meadow he will purify himself and hide his sword, with which he slew the cattle; no good has come to him from the Greeks since Hector gave it to him. For the future, he will know how to revere the sons of Atreus (Agamemnon and Menelaus) and yield to the gods, as winter yields to summer, sleep to waking. He too will be self-restrained, *sophron*. He will be aware that friends and enemies may change places. Telling Tecmessa to pray that his wish be accomplished, he exits, and the chorus sings in joy. But now a messenger enters (719), to say that Teucer, who had been away on a raid, has returned. The Greeks met him with hostility, but the prophet Calchas in friendship warned him that Ajax must stay indoors one day, while the anger of the goddess lasts. He twice offended Athena: on leaving Salamis he ignored his father's advice to seek victory with the gods' help, for even a weakling could win if gods aid him—he could win alone; and when Athena came to encourage him in battle, he told her to help others, for his place in the battleline would not break.

All exit to find Teucer and Ajax. Ajax enters alone—the scene has become the meadow by the sea (815). He fixes the sword in the earth and prays that Teucer prevent his body from being thrown to the dogs and birds, that he have an easy journey to the Underworld, that the Furies avenge his death, and that the Sun tell his parents. He falls on the sword, and chorus and Tecmessa enter to find him and lament. Teucer enters (974) and foresees how his father will blame him for his brother's death.[6] Ajax, he says, was slain by the dead Hector through the sword, as Hector was dragged to his death, tied to Achilles' chariot by the strap given him by Ajax. He sends Tecmessa to bring the child.

Menelaus enters to forbid the burial of Ajax (1047). As Ajax was excessive, so now it is his turn to be proud, and he will rule at least the dead Ajax. Teucer denies that Ajax was subordinate to Menelaus. The two wrangle over the justice of the award of arms and whether the gods would want Ajax to be buried, and the scene ends with the two exchanging threatening insults thinly disguised as fables. Tecmessa returns, and she and the boy sit as suppliants by the body. The chorus sings again of the misery of the war, even worse now without Ajax.

Agamemnon enters (1226), denying that Ajax was a greater warrior than himself, and calling Teucer a bastard, a slave, and a barbarian (his mother was a Trojan captive). Order will disappear if he gives way to such a one. Teucer names Ajax's greatest deeds, which Agamemnon could not equal, and evokes Agamemnon's barbarian ancestry and adulterous mother. As violence threatens, Odysseus enters (1318), and argues for Ajax's burial. He was the best of the Greeks, and excellence overcomes hate; to insult the dead is impious, and Odysseus sees that no mortal should dishonor the dead. Agamemnon gives way as a favor to Odysseus, though he insists as he exits on his hatred for Ajax; Odysseus wishes to join in Ajax's funeral. Teucer praises him while cursing Atreus's sons, but shrinks from allowing Odysseus to help in preparing Ajax for burial, lest the dead be displeased. The play ends as Ajax is carried off in procession.

Ajax and the *Iliad*[7]

The Ajax of this play is not a character with whom we find it easy to feel sympathy. His willingness to murder because his honor has been slighted is not the result of his madness, for the madness was the divine mechanism which frustrated his intention. In the play he first appears carrying the whip with which he has been torturing a ram he thinks is Odysseus, while his second entry is made sitting in a pool of bloody corpses. He is harsh toward Tecmessa. Yet with the horror generated by the spectacle of Ajax is a genuine pity. The audience is directed to pity Ajax from the first by the response of Odysseus. From the initial exchange with Athena we know that Odysseus and Ajax are enemies, so that his response is defined as that of a hostile observer. When the goddess makes Odysseus invisible, and calls Ajax forth in order that Odysseus may tell the Greeks what he has seen (66–67), Odysseus is made, in effect, the audience for a play-within-a-play, whose reaction is a guide. When, therefore, he rejects Athena's suggestion that he laugh at his humiliated enemy, as Ajax laughs over his imagined victim Odysseus, and instead announces his pity (121), we cannot but realize that pity is the human response to such a sight. Ajax is gleefully cruel, but we cannot be certain how much of this is his madness, how much the real Ajax; the intent to murder need not imply this horrible gloating. And Athena is even crueller than Ajax, playing with her victim's belief that she is his ally. The end of the scene defines the earlier Ajax in terms which establish him as a model: inferior to none in either foresight or in ability to perform appropriate action. The latter term suggests a great deal: the excellence of Ajax was not apparently confined to war, nor was it a simple, heroic, inflexibility. To do what the occasion demands encompasses the whole of *arete*, the aristocratic ideal of excellence in every sphere. It is surely deliberate that Athena's description of what Ajax was echoes, in its division of good sense and proper action, Hector's praise of Ajax as both sensible and mighty at the end of their inconclusive duel in the *Iliad* (7. 288–89). This encounter, with its air of chivalry, may symbolize what Ajax was; yet he and his brother regard that very chivalry, marked by the exchange of gifts between the two enemies, as a cause of the downfall of Ajax.

In the first part of the play, the issue of the attempt to kill the chiefs is suppressed. Ajax himself does not regret it, but is grieved only by his humiliating failure. Such revenge, which requites a mere insult with death, belongs to the Homeric world. It is not, however, a goal we would associate with Homer's Ajax, but with his Achilles, whose anger is so strong that it does not allow him to accept the convincing plea of Ajax. In the initial quarrel between Achilles and Agamemnon in the *Iliad,* the king announces that he will take

Achilles' prize of honor to replace his own, which he is being forced to surrender. Achilles draws his sword, hesitating whether to kill Agamemnon or restrain himself, when Athena appears to restrain him, invisible to all but himself (1. 188–218). Yet his rage fulfills itself by a withdrawal from battle which leads to the deaths of his own comrades. It is this anger which Sophocles has given his hero, and he relies in part on the sympathy the epic has already created for the excessive and destructive rage of Achilles to define his protagonist. There is a certain rightness in Achilles' arms serving to motivate an anger like his own. But Achilles had divine support in his wrath; Athena stopped him by a promise of future compensation. Athena had a grudge against Ajax, and her intervention was disastrous for him. Gods, however, generally intervene only in accordance with human character, so that Ajax's suffering cannot simply be blamed on Athena: it is notable that he tried to take his revenge at night, by craft—a method which violated his own nature.

When the revenge is finally argued by Teucer against Agamemnon and Menelaus, the kings weaken their own case by themselves seeking revenge on the dead Ajax. They also assert their own authority, describing Ajax as a disobedient subordinate. Teucer answers that Ajax came to Troy in obedience to his oath, not to Menelaus or for Helen's sake (1097–1114). This is the oath of Helen's suitors, wherein all promised to defend the man chosen to marry her (Menelaus, as it turned out). Teucer's claim is evidently based on Achilles' statement in the same scene of the *Iliad* already echoed (1. 149–71) that he owes no obedience to Agamemnon; he came to Troy as a favor to him, and will not remain to be dishonored. Again there is a similarity and a difference. Achilles did not take the oath—he was only a child when Helen was married—and came to Troy to seek glory for himself. Hence the argument is sounder for him than for Ajax. Yet Teucer recalls the truth that the chiefs in Homer are only *primi inter pares;* Agamemnon is commander in chief and leads the largest contingent, but he is not the overlord of the other kings.

Ajax is thus set against the Homeric Achilles, as he is against the former self evoked at the close of the prologue. Homer's Ajax, the loyal defender with the great shield, often seems remote from Sophocles' character, though the Sophoclean Ajax has done the deeds recounted of him by Homer; the profound attachment to the community is inverted, appearing only as resentment of that community's failure to honor him. The isolation of Ajax is underlined by

the third of the Homeric reminiscences, in which Ajax is shadowed
by Hector. The scene in which Ajax bids farewell to his son (545–
77) is obviously modeled on the famed passage in the sixth book
of the *Iliad* in which Hector says good-bye to his wife and son.
Each detail is a careful contrast. Hector's child cries in fear at his
father's helmet, while Ajax is sure that his son will not fear the
gore with which he is spattered, and apparently he does not. Hector
prays that his son be like him among the Trojans, and that someone
say "He is by far better than his father"; Ajax prays only that his
son be luckier than himself, but otherwise the same. Hector foresees
evil for his wife and child, while Ajax is confident that Teucer will
protect his. Ajax is prouder than Hector. But perhaps more important is the contrast in situation. Hector is the father of a legitimate child within a stable, though threatened city. He goes to his
death for his honor but also in defense of his home. Ajax is far from
his native land—the chorus constantly expresses homesickness—
and isolated from the only community he has, the army. His child
is the son of a captive. Hence he is both fiercer and yet closer to
his son than Hector: he envies the boy his lack of understanding.
When the child grows up, he must show his father's enemies who
he is, but in the meanwhile let him "feed on light breezes." Hector
imagines the mother's rejoicing when her son comes from battle
with bloody spoils, while Ajax sees him as his mother's joy in the
immediate future (559). Hector's prayer assumes Troy's survival,
despite his presentiments, and is not fated to be fulfilled. Ajax is
more realistic, in spite of his perhaps misplaced confidence in Teucer.

Hybris and Sophrosyne

One last Homeric echo stands out among these complex recol-
lections: the remarks of Ajax which precipitated Athena's anger are
evidently based on the boast of the protagonist's namesake, the
Lesser Ajax, at *Odyssey* 4. 504. This echo, however, can only be
understood in the context of the themes of *hybris* and *sophrosyne,*
which some scholars have tried to make the center of the play, while
others have largely ignored them. Ajax was guilty of pride toward
the goddess *(hybris),* thus showing his lack of the virtue of self-
restraint and good sense, *sophrosyne.* His destruction is the inevitable
result of his offense; he is an object-lesson in conventional Greek
morality. This is one interpretation of the play, and the work does,

in two passages, directly invite this interpretation: the theme is too explicit to be ignored, yet too confined to dominate.[8]

The first of these passages is, of course, the end of the prologue, where Athena points the moral of Ajax's fall. Odysseus's pity defines mortals as "images" or "shadows" without substance: this attitude of helplessness before divine power is the essence of *sophrosyne*. Athena then warns him not to be proud toward the gods because of might or money. The gods love those who have *sophrosyne* but hate the *kakoi*, the bad. The exact application of this moral is hard to define. Ajax, whose fall proves divine power, ought to be the figure described—Odysseus is being warned against Ajax's sins. But the lines do not completely fit him. He has boasted of strength, we will later learn, but was not an especially wealthy hero. Odysseus was not one of the richest leaders at Troy either, so that this feature is not there as a special warning to him. Furthermore, the man of *sophrosyne* is not usually the opposite of the *kakos*. The latter term implies the lack of aristocratic virtue or stature—low birth, cowardice, and meanness of spirit are components of *kakia*. Ajax's offenses against *sophrosyne*, however, are excesses of aristocratic pride. The only sense in which he could easily be called "base" is in reference to his present degradation as a mad outcast, and if that is the sense the statement means nothing: it is obvious that "the gods hate the miserable," for they would not be miserable otherwise. Rather, the moral is inspired by Ajax, but not confined to his case or even put in a form that closely fits him. It tells Odysseus what he can learn from Ajax's fall, without saying very much about Ajax's own case, and through its reference to the arrogance of wealth prepares for the sons of Atreus, who exemplify the arrogance of wealth and power. Odysseus is the prudent man, whom the gods love, and the sons of Atreus may well be base men, whom they hate. Ajax is neither one nor the other; the gods have punished him, but the prologue leaves his final relation to them in doubt.

Although it is clear from the prologue that Ajax must have committed some offense of pride against the gods, what he did is not specified until the messenger's speech. We then learn that he rejected the gods' help. There is no doubt that this was impious, but it should be judged by comparison with the model of Ajax's sin: the Lesser Ajax boasted that he had escaped the sea *against the will* of the gods. Sophocles' Ajax does not suggest that the gods can be defied, but desires a success which is owed not to them, but to his inherited excellence, his *physis*. Ironically, he has for once accepted the help of Athena in the attack on the chiefs, to his ruin; he cannot, in fact, accept divine help and live. Yet if we look at the position of the messenger's speech, Athena's anger becomes mysterious. Ajax has left after the speech which convinces his friends that he has softened (the "deception-speech"). Now the messenger says that he may be saved if he is kept within, for the anger of the goddess will only last one day. Ajax has claimed that he will "purify" himself and escape the anger of the goddess (656). If her anger is to last only one day, it appears that he will escape her anger truly, but in death. We do not know how Athena's anger affects Ajax, for his death is entirely sane, but Ajax sees his death as a reconciliation with the gods, and the reconciliation is successful. It is not an atonement, and Ajax is not penitent: his suicide is what he chooses, and it also solves the gods' hostility. In fact, the messenger ensures that the friends of Ajax will find him before his enemies, and thus helps grant the prayer Ajax has not yet made.

Ajax says in the "deception-speech" that he will learn *sophrosyne* (677), and evokes the cycles of nature as a model for his learning to yield. In some sense, death renders him *sophron* and thus, perhaps, loved instead of hated by the gods. In the second part, Menelaus calls on cyclic order to defend his own arrogance and impiety (1087–88): "Formerly this man was blazing and full of *hybris,* but now I am proud." The chorus immediately points out how illogically he blames Ajax for a *hybris* he imitates. Agamamnon likewise misapplies the morality of restraint in arguing that Teucer's defense of the dead Ajax is *hybris* (1258) and that he must learn *sophrosyne* (1259); his *sophrosyne* is slavery, and his dismissal of Ajax as "a shadow by now" is controverted by Odysseus's recognition in the prologue that all men are shadows. And Odysseus, in the end, shows that he has understood what *sophrosyne* means, when he insists on the burial of Ajax in recognition of the common human condition. Thus the theme binds the opening and conclusion: Odysseus gains from the sight of the madness of Ajax that understanding of human weakness which enjoins the decent treatment of Ajax dead.

Unity

Sophrosyne is one of several themes which bind together the halves of a drama whose unity is much disputed. For many, the play loses tension once Ajax is dead.[9] However we decide the question of its unity, the structure must be recognized. All three early Sophoclean tragedies—*Ajax, Trachiniae,* and *Antigone*—can be called "diptychs," plays which are formed of two readily distinct parts. In the case of *Ajax,* this division is highly formalized.

In only one other surviving Greek tragedy do we have a change of scene and an exit and reentrance of the chorus, Aeschylus's *Eumenides.* In *Ajax,* the chorus exits after the messenger-speech, and the stage is bare. When Ajax enters, the scene has become a lonely place by the shore, while the following monologue is exceptional, since very rarely, except in a prologue, does an actor deliver a speech truly alone. His speech is followed by the reentry of the chorus, as if the play were beginning again. *Ajax* thus not only has two dramatic parts, one treating the process which leads to the protagonist's death, the other to his burial, but two formal parts. Even if we regard this structure as a mistake aesthetically, the second half is not just an epilogue: we are encouraged to see it as almost a new play. Yet it should be noticed that the second half begins with the suicide of Ajax, not after it; his speech is both the conclusion of the first section and the opening of the second. This "bridge" speech is therefore critical to understanding the relation between the first and second halves.

Why, then, a second drama devoted to the burial of Ajax? To say that Greeks cared deeply about the burial of the dead is a commonplace, true but not really an explanation. A further issue has often been raised in the case of Ajax, who was a hero at Athens. A hero, *hērōs,* in the Greek sense of the word is a dead person with power to help or harm the living, particularly in the area of his grave.[10] Heroes had to be propitiated by offerings at their graves, for they were dangerous when not placated. Although many of the epic heroes were also cult heroes, not all were, and many cult heroes had no legend. Many indeed were nameless—the discovery of an already ancient tomb could lead to a cult of the anonymous hero buried there. One of the ten Athenian tribes was named after Ajax, and he was supposed to have given his help during the battle of Salamis. The burial of Ajax may have appealed to Attic patriotism. Many critics have argued that Ajax has to be "rehabilitated" by the dispute over burial in order to satisfy Athenian sensibilities. But there is no evidence that human virtues were expected of a hero, nor is patriotic sentiment enough to justify the elaboration of the second part.

But the cult of Ajax is important. Just after his entrance, Teucer sends Tecmessa to fetch Ajax's son (985–89). When the two enter, after the dispute with Menelaus, he places them by the corpse as suppliants (1168–84), and this tableau stands in the background throughout the final scene. The suppliant, like the hero, has a defined place in Greek religion; by carrying certain tokens and performing specific actions he puts himself under divine protection, so that injury to him is sacrilege. In this scene the corpse of Ajax plays the role of an altar or sacred place, and the locks of hair dedicated in mourning replace boughs or fillets. The suppliancy is intended to give Ajax the protection of the suppliants and yet to give the suppliants his protection: his burial is endangered, and yet his body is treated as though he were already a hero, with the ability to shelter a suppliant.[11] Ajax seems to be at once the utterly vulnerable mortal and, in some sense, the powerful presence below. But this paradox leads to another which has already been mentioned, that the burial of Ajax is not brought about by Teucer or by the suppliants, but by Odysseus: yet the education of Odysseus is itself the work of the spectacle of Ajax provided by Athena. The hint of divine protection given by the tableau is true in another sense, and when Ajax in his madness calls Athena his "ally" in the prologue the irony is highly complex: by no means his ally in the form he thinks, she is in fact his ally in arousing the pity of Odysseus. The drama is about Ajax, living and dead, in relation to men and to gods.

Vision

The prologue establishes a complex relationship of vision and invisibility. Athena is invisible to Odysseus, but there is no sign that Ajax does not see her.[12] On the other hand, Ajax is prevented from seeing Odysseus. When the events of the prologue are described by Tecmessa, it is clear that she saw nothing but shadows (301) and thought Ajax was speaking to himself. That Odysseus, the favorite of the goddess, does not see her, implies that the actual sight of the goddess is perhaps to be avoided; Ajax is intimate with the divinity, but this intimacy is his destruction. Yet it is a real intimacy. The final words of Ajax in the prologue are a request that

Athena always be such an ally to him (116–17), and the messenger-
speech, which gives her wrath a place among the causes of his death,
marks the fulfillment of his request. Recovering from his madness,
he fully knows what part Athena has played (401–3, 450–56). But
he does not know that Odysseus is not mocking (379–81). Odysseus
has contact with the divine only insofar as the gods can bring him
to an understanding of humanity. Ajax is close to the gods, but has
no understanding of other men; he misjudges Odysseus, overesti-
mates Teucer, and surprises himself.

At 589–90 Ajax insists that he owes the gods nothing, and warns
Tecmessa that she is a fool if she thinks she can educate him now
(594–95). He is resolved on suicide. Yet when he emerges from
his tent at the opening of the next scene (646) he has, to his surprise,
changed: he now feels pity for his wife and child. In the great
"deception-speech" he continues to speak of his death, but in very
different terms. It now appears as an attempt at reconciliation with
the gods and as a purification rite; Tecmessa and the chorus imagine,
as they are surely intended to imagine, that Ajax has abandoned his
purpose. This speech has caused much controversy.[13] Many critics
have been unwilling to believe that Ajax intends deceit, arguing
that this deceit is contrary to his nature; so it is, but he has already
left that nature in the crafty attack on the chiefs. On the other
hand, many have asked why, if he seeks to deceive, he uses language
which barely conceals the truth. Two answers may be given to this
question: both that the equivocation of the speech does represent
an important inner truth—death is a reconciliation with the gods—
and that prophetic speech is a characteristic of those near death, so
that he is almost incapable of saying anything which is not, in some
sense, true—the riddle of his words is akin to the riddles of an
oracle.[14] The speech is extremely difficult not only because its significance lies on so many levels but also because it is not entirely
coherent.

Ajax speaks of going to the bathing-places by the sea in order to
purify himself and escape the goddess's wrath. There he will hide
the sword Hector gave him, for no goodwill has come to him from
the Greeks since he received it. He will learn to yield to the gods
and revere the sons of Atreus. Snowy winter gives way to summer,
night to day, and he too will learn *sophrosyne*. From now on he will
hate an enemy only to the extent of realizing he may become a
friend, and vice versa; all this will come out well. And they may

hear that Ajax is saved. That Ajax sees his death as a purification is understandable. But he also links it with the cycles of change in nature, even including sleep, which loosens the one it has bound. Ajax is in one sense yielding to change, accepting it as the way of the world, and the images he chooses for change recognize it as benign. But his death will not place him among ever-recurring cycles, but rather give him permanence. He will no longer interfere with the sons of Atreus, and he is certainly giving way to the gods, since he thinks they wish his death, and that he is thus acting in harmony with them. But how will he revere the sons of Atreus, whom he curses just before his death? The word is surely sarcastic, and the line ambiguous even within an ambiguous speech; "I will learn to revere them," he says—but the dead learn nothing, and the Greek verb can equally mean "learn *how* to"—the curse is perhaps the form of reverence appropriate to them. Yet in this same speech Ajax claims to understand that both friendship and enmity are unstable, even as he blames his trouble with the Greeks on the sword he received from Hector. The sword is evidently the symbol of unalterable hostility. Hector and Ajax, in exchanging gifts, acted as though hatred could be limited and did not even preclude a certain friendship, and both were destroyed by the exchange, as we later learn from Teucer. So to reconcile the sword with Ajax's words on friendship is not easy: perhaps the principle of restrained friendship and enmity is true, but not for Ajax; his friendship with an enemy led to hatred between himself and his former friends. Or it may be true, but only in a world Ajax wishes to leave. His statement that "for most, friendship is an unsafe harbor" (682–83) points to the future friendship of Odysseus—he will find a harbor in a friend he thought an enemy.

The deception-speech is the center of the play. Ajax must die, for he cannot live in humiliation and remain Ajax. In this speech he transforms his death from a rejection of the changefulness of human life to an acceptance of it, from the result of being hated by the gods to an acceptance of them. He goes to die, not in the darkness of the tent, but in the light. His comment on being saved is prophetic. The following messenger-speech confirms the meaning of his choice. Calchas says that Ajax may live if he can be kept within his tent this one day, while Athena is angry. The prophecy comes too late to save Ajax in the sense in which salvation is understood by the messenger (779). But it makes the self-chosen death

of Ajax also the fulfillment of Athena's anger, and makes it clear
that he will be, in some sense, saved, for her anger will not outlast
the day. His decision to leave the tent, which required that his
definition of his choice serve to deceive his followers, is shown to
represent the only way he could die. The prophet raises the possibility that Ajax might live, but life is not what Ajax wants, and
the prophecy shows that he has known without being told how to
obtain the death desired. Moreover, the same speech in which Calchas depicts the limited anger of the goddess shows the rage of the
Greeks, and Calchas in no way implies that Ajax will certainly
survive if he lives through this day: both Ajax and his followers
anticipate the worst at the hands of the army, and the messenger-
speech, describing Teucer's hostile reception, shows that this is
reasonable. Ajax dies while his death still belongs to the gods. The
death of Ajax is caused by Athena and by the dead Hector, but
these are causes of his choice. And in his last speech, his vision
becomes effectual prayer.

The Second Play

The second half of the play makes sense only in the context of
the harmony between Ajax and his goddess-destroyer. The final
speech of Ajax (815–65) is mainly a series of prayers. He asks Zeus
that Teucer may be the finder of his body, so as to save him from
being thrown to scavenger animals, and to Hermes for a quick death;
he asks the sun to report his death to his parents. He also calls on
the spirits of vengeance, the Furies, to attack the sons of Atreus
and the armies. The prayer to the sun cannot be answered within
the play. But the answering of the other prayers is the impulse of
the second half of the drama. Ajax has a special power to bless and
curse, but the flawed and mortal Ajax does not leave the drama.
As with his death, events following the death of Ajax have both
natural and supernatural motivations.

The prayer for Teucer's rapid arrival is fulfilled, but although
Ajax can pray effectually, he does not guess that Teucer may not
be able to protect him. At Odysseus's entry, it appears that Teucer
may die in defense of his brother without saving him. But in de-
bating Agamemnon and Menelaus on their own terms, crudely but
effectively, he causes them to damn themselves ethically, and creates
a tumult which prompts Odysseus's entrance. He also builds the

tableau which hints at Ajax's heroic power; yet this tableau has no visible effect on the action. The burial of Ajax is secured on the purely human level, by the intervention of a humane Odysseus. But we know that his humanity is the result of what a goddess shows him in the prologue, and the apparently ineffectual efforts of Teucer may play a hidden part.

Conspicuously, Odysseus is absent from the final curse of Ajax, although Ajax does not know that Odysseus will help him: the curse, like the deception-speech, is mysteriously guided. Odysseus also finally bestows on Ajax the praise for lack of which he died: he states that, after Achilles, he was the best of the Greeks (1340–41), and so symbolically retracts the Judgment of the Arms. This shift marks how the second half of the play recalls the essence of what happened before it began. The sons of Atreus try to dishonor Ajax, and in their debate with Teucer both reveal the impossibility of fair judgment from such men and also further confirm the accuracy of the dead man's curse. Agamemnon and Menelaus are virtually identical characters. Menelaus insults Teucer as a bowman; Agamemnon, as a bastard; Menelaus speaks of Ajax as if he had been a common soldier instead of a king, Agamemnon as if the deeds of Ajax did not surpass his own. The tension is higher in the second dispute not because the arguments are at a higher level, but because the suppliant tableau now stands behind the disputants, a reminder at once of the common humanity of the dead and of the potential power of Ajax. When the drama ends with the funeral procession, the prayers of Ajax have been fulfilled. The sons of Atreus have shown themselves more given to *hybris* than was Ajax, and so promised the fulfillment of the curse—which is duly repeated by Teucer (1389–92). Odysseus is not allowed to join in the actual preparation of the body for burial, but he will join in the funeral itself. Ajax cannot be brought back into the human community; but what is best in the human world will attend him with respect.

Chapter Three

A Deceptive World:
Women of Trachis

The Plot

The story of *Women of Trachis* is simple: a woman, Deianeira, learns
that her husband, the great hero Heracles, loves another woman.
She sends him a robe annoited with what she thinks is a love potion.
It is poisonous, and causes his death. She kills herself. The drama
begins as Deianeira tells her life story: she was courted by a river-
god, Achelous; at last Heracles defeated the river in a fight for her.
But her married life has been miserable, since he is always away,
rarely even seeing his own children. Since he killed Iphitus, son of
King Eurytus of Oechalia on the island of Euboea, the family has
lived in exile in Trachis. Now Heracles has been gone fifteen months;
no word of him has come. He left a writing-tablet with Deianeira;
its message frightens her. A nurse has been listening, and she in-
tervenes to suggest that Deianeira send her son Hyllus to seek news.
Opportunely Hyllus comes from the house (1.58). He has some word
already: for a year Heracles was enslaved to Omphale, queen of
Lydia. Now he is besieging Oechalia. Deianeira is alarmed, for she
has a prophecy that a struggle there is crucial for Heracles. Either
he will die, or live happily hereafter. Hyllus goes out on his mission
(92–93).

The chorus of local young women enters. They sing of how grief
and joy alternate in life, and good luck may come. Heracles is son
of Zeus, who will be mindful of him. But Deianeira replies that in
their happy innocence they cannot understand her suffering. When
Heracles left her, he told her his will in the case of his death and
gave her a tablet containing the oracle given him by Zeus at Dodona:
at the end of fifteen months he would either die or be untroubled
henceforth.

A messenger enters (180) to say that he has heard the herald
Lichas announcing to the people that Heracles is alive and victorious.

27

Deianeira prompts the chorus to sing for joy. Lichas enters (229) with a train of captive women. Heracles himself is still in Euboea, he explains, preparing a sacrifice to Zeus at Cape Cenaeum, across the Malian Gulf from Trachis. The women are captives from Oechalia, selected by Heracles for himself and the gods. Heracles spent a year as Omphale's slave as a punishment, decreed by Zeus, for the killing of Iphitus; Heracles has avenged his humiliation by sacking the city of Iphitus's father. When Heracles visited Eurytus, his host insulted him, calling him an archer inferior to his (Eurytus's) sons and a slave (because he performed labors for Eurystheus of Argos). Eurytus threw the drunken Heracles out of his house. In revenge Heracles murdered Iphitus when the latter came to Heracles' city, Tiryns, looking for some lost cattle. Zeus was angered by the crafty form the vengeance took (for Heracles crept up behind his victim to push him over a wall) and so demanded the service to Omphale.

Deianeira pities one of the maidens especially, for her bearing is noble, but Lichas denies knowing who she is, and the girl is silent. Lichas and the train enter the house (334). The messenger explains that Lichas has lied, for earlier he told everyone that Heracles loved this maiden, Iole, daughter of Eurytus, and took the city for her. When her father refused to give her to Heracles as a concubine, Heracles had concocted a "small pretext." Lichas comes out (393) and the truth is wrested from him by Deianeira's statement that she understands the power of love and does not blame Heracles or Iole. Deianeira promises Lichas gifts for Heracles in return for those he has sent, and they enter the house; the chorus sings of the power of Aphrodite, using as an example Heracles' battle with Achelous.

Deianeira explains to the chorus that she cannot bear the situation; though she is not angry, she cannot share her own marriage-bed with a younger woman. Long ago, the centaur Nessus carried her over the River Evenus. He caressed her, and Heracles shot him with the bow; but he told Deianeira to collect his blood where the poisoned arrow had struck him: it would be a charm, so that Heracles would love no woman more than herself. Now she has anointed a robe with the charm, and will use it, if the chorus agrees. Covering the robe under seal, she gives it to Lichas for Heracles to wear for the first time at the sacrifice. He exits (632), and the chorus imagines Heracles' splendid return. But Deianeira returns in alarm. The bit of wool with which she applied the charm has melted away, and she has realized that Nessus would not have meant well. But if Heracles dies, so will she. Hyllus enters (734). His mother has murdered his father. Heracles put on the robe, which clung to him when the ritual fire warmed it, so that he was wracked with pain; he threw Lichas over a cliff. Heracles screamed and cursed, rolling in agony. Now he has been ferried over the gulf, and will soon arrive. Hyllus prays that Justice and the Fury punish his mother; she exits in silence. The chorus sings of how Heracles was to find an end to his labors after fifteen years: so it will be, for the dead have rest. This is the work of Aphrodite.

Cries come from within, and the Nurse appears (871). Deianeira has killed herself. First she took a tearful farewell of her house, then sat on her marriage-bed. The Nurse fetched Hyllus, but when they entered the bedroom, Deianeira had plunged a sword into her side. Hyllus cried, realizing that he had been unjust. The chorus sings of the double grief of the house.

Heracles is brought in on a litter (971). Despite the warning of the old man who attends the bearers, Hyllus laments, and awakens his sleeping father. Heracles screams to be killed, and uncovers himself so that Hyllus may see the effects of the robe. He addresses his arms, which destroyed so many monsters; if Deianeira would come into his grasp, he would end his career of punishing evildoers by killing her. Hyllus tells him what has happened. Heracles now says he must die. Zeus prophesied to him that one no longer living would kill him, and Nessus is his slayer. The oracle promising him rest is also fulfilled, since the dead have no labor. After extracting an oath from Hyllus that he will do what his father orders, he commands him to build a pyre on the summit of Mt. Oeta and burn him on it. Hyllus is horrified; eventually they agree that Hyllus will do everthing but light the pyre. Heracles has another demand: Hyllus must marry Iole. Again he is horrified, but yields, calling on the gods to witness that his motive is filial piety. Heracles is carried out in funeral procession, as Hyllus accuses the gods of not caring for their children. In the last lines he speaks of the recent terrible sufferings the chorus has seen, "And nothing of these which is not Zeus."[1]

Date and Sources

The dating of this play has been a subject of long and perplexed controversy.[2] The majority of scholars are now agreed in ranking it with *Ajax* and *Antigone* as one of the earlier group of surviving plays. Like these it has a "diptych" structure, falling into two quite distinct parts. It also shows the earlier Sophoclean method of character portrayal: Deianeira's major changes of mind take place offstage and are reported, while the later dramas present characters struggling with decisions on stage. The problem of dating is a serious one, because it cannot be detached from problems of source and literary influence.

There was an epic called *The Capture of Oechalia*, attributed to Homer or one Creophylus, which told the story of Iole. The treacherous murder of Iphitus is mentioned at *Odyssey* 21. 24–30. Clearly also the story of Heracles' service to Omphale was famous (Ion of Chios wrote a satyr-play on the subject), although probably Sophocles first connected this story with that of Oechalia. What we do not know is how the stories of Deianeira and Iole were first joined, or how Deianeira was portrayed in earlier literature. The poisoned garment and the role of Lichas are mentioned in surviving fragments of the Hesiodic *Catalogue of Women* (fr. 25. 20–25 M–W), and the death of Nessus was described by the archaic poet Archilochus and in a lyric fragment of unknown authorship.[3] In the fifth poem of Bacchylides, composed in 476, Heracles on his journey to the Underworld meets the hero Meleager, whose own mother caused his death. Heracles asks whether Meleager left alive an unmarried sister, and Meleager tells him of his sister Deianeira. The parallel is obvious: Heracles will be killed by his jealous wife, as Meleager was by his angry mother.

On the other hand, Bacchylides 16 tells the story in a pathetic style (24–35):

Then an unconquerable god wove a tearful plan for Deianeira, when she heard the painful message that the warrior son of Zeus was sending home white-armed Iole as a wife. Unlucky, miserable, what she contrived! Mighty resentment was her ruin, and the dark veil over the future, when by the rosy Lycorma she received from Nessus a divine, uncanny gift.[4]

This version is close to Sophocles' in both plot and mood. If Sophocles influenced Bacchylides directly, *Women of Trachis* would probably have to be a very early play, from the 450s (Bacchylides' last dated work comes from 452). Clearly, Sophocles is not following the allusive narrative of Bacchylides. But our ignorance of the Heracles epics of Peisander and Panyassis does not allow judgment, since both Sophocles and Bacchylides could be developing an epic model.

Bacchylides' version does not imply a meeting of the rivals for Heracles' love.[5] Their encounter in Sophocles is based on another meeting between a wife and a concubine, that of Clytemnestra and Cassandra in Aeschylus's *Agamemnon*.[6] Cassandra is Agamemnon's special prize from the Trojan War, and Clytemnestra, the wife of Agamemnon, tries to persuade her to follow him into the house. Cassandra, however, stands mutely on stage. When Clytemnestra (who the audience knows is planning to murder her husband) goes inside, Cassandra delivers a long prophecy, which includes her own death. At last she enters of her own will, and Clytemnestra later boasts of killing her as a "relish" to the murder of Agamemnon. As Achilles and Hector served as foil for Ajax, Clytemnestra and Cassandra serve as foil for Deianeira and Iole. Both Deianeira and Clytemnestra kill their husbands, but Deianeira does so unintentionally. Although, unlike her model, she is faithful, she does not blame her husband for his infidelity or hate his mistress. On the contrary, she pities her on first sight. Likewise, the silence of Iole is modeled on that of Cassandra. Cassandra's silence, however, is a mere preparation for her speech. She understands events better than anyone else in the play, but speaks only when she chooses. Iole never speaks; her character appears only through Deianeira's interpretation of her silence as a sign of nobility and pathos. Yet while she takes no action, she is destined to marry and establish a dynasty.

The echo is visual, and has sometimes been thought to point to a date not too long after *Agamemnon,* produced in 458; but Aeschylus's masterpiece was an immediate classic, and comic parodies long after original performances suggest that the Greek audience had a good memory. The opening scene of *Women of Trachis* recalls the *Odyssey* and perhaps another epic about Odysseus, the *Telegony* (from which Sophocles derived a tragedy).[7] Deianeira shares the fear and passivity of Penelope, though she does send Hyllus, at the Nurse's suggestion, to seek word of his father, while Hyllus's model, Telemachus, slips away on his quest at divine prompting without telling his mother. This model will be proved wrong: instead of an Odysseus who has to deal with Penelope's suitors, the sexual tension will surround the husband, and the drama does not tend to a happy reunion of its separated couple. The echo rightly determines, however, the basic story-type of the plot—the audience can realize from the start that this is a story of return. Heracles, like Odysseus, is a famous hero who will come home after many trials.

So much of the play's context is clear. There are also links, however, with Euripides, Sophocles' younger contemporary. Unlike any other surviving Sophoclean play, this one begins with a long speech, addressed in effect to the audience, and describing the antecedents of the plot in the Euripidean manner. Though Deianeira's monologue is closely attached to the Nurse's intervention, while Euripides characteristically sets his prologue-speech apart, the opening does seem to reflect his style. Here the direction of influence is clear. Euripides' *Medea* of 431 has a poisoned robe whose effects resemble the one of this play, while his *Heracles* (ca. 418) has a sleeping entrance which can be compared to Heracles' sleeping entrance in *Women of Trachis*. But the poisoned robe may have been an established motif with traditional details, and it cannot be proved which tragedian, if either, borrowed the sleeping Heracles.

Most interesting, perhaps, are the comparisons with *Alcestis* (438) and *Hippolytus*. Alcestis has assumed her husband's fate of an early death. The play is set on the day she is fated to die; a slave describes how she bade farewell to her household and particularly her marriage-bed. The similarity to Deianeira's farewell to her home and marriage is very strong, but the direction of influence is, as usual, hard to determine, and we may again be dealing with a traditional motif. Both passages are dramatically effective in very different ways. Set against the Euripidean parallel, the intense sexuality of Deianeira's death scene becomes even sharper. Alcestis, who is not a victim of erotic passion, does not actually die upon her bed. If *Alcestis* is the model, the scene is another example of Sophocles' characteristic use of earlier literature as foil: the pathos and irony of Deianeira's death are deepened if she acts before her death exactly as a woman would who has saved her husband, rather than killed him. Deianeira is a would-be Alcestis.

Structure

This drama, like *Ajax*, has a "diptych" structure, falling, as we earlier remarked, into two sections. Deianeira, the protagonist of the first part, is scarcely mentioned in the last three hundred lines, while a new character, Heracles, dominates the stage. Of course the arrival of Heracles has been the goal of all the earlier action, but the impression of discontinuity is still jarring.

Here a last comparison with Euripides may be helpful. The *Hippolytus* of 428 has likewise two main characters. Phaedra loves her stepson, Hippolytus. Her nurse wins her permission to "cure" her magically; the cure is a solicitation of the young man, who is devoted to chastity. Phaedra overhears his furious tirade against her, and kills herself, leaving a note in which she claims he raped her. Unwilling to break the oath of secrecy the nurse had extracted from him, Hippolytus is cursed by his father, and dies. This work is also both a diptych and a tragedy of *eros*. The first half is given to Phaedra and her attempts to overcome her passion, the second to Hippolytus and the false accusation. Like Deianeira and Heracles, they never meet, and utterly fail to understand each other, Hippolytus assuming that Phaedra sent the nurse, Phaedra that Hippolytus will violate his oath and betray her. The lack of contact underscores the lack of understanding. *Women of Trachis* employs the same method. Heracles and Deianeira never meet on stage because they do not meet at all. Instead they communicate through inadequate intermediaries—the writing-tablet with the oracle, Lichas, Hyllus, the robe. This is a tragedy of garbled messages.

The two protagonists belong almost to different worlds. Deianeira lives entirely within the world of women, the house, while Heracles occupies the public world; Deianeira responds to Iole differently from any earlier mistress of Heracles in part because the relationship invades her own realm. Ideally, a marriage allows the two spheres to unite through reciprocity. When Odysseus and Penelope are reunited in *Odyssey* 23, they follow their sexual union by telling each other their stories (300–341). She endured at home, he wandering, but the exchange of stories marks the sympathetic participation of each in the other's adventures. Marriage, like all relationships in Greek ethics, depends on the participants' reciprocal and benevolent exchange. In *Women of Trachis,* all exchanges are corrupt.

Typically, a gift from the antecedents of the drama is both the cause and the paradigm for the gift-giving at the center of the plot. Nessus tried to rape Deianeira, and death was his return. But Nessus also made a corresponding return, his blood mixed with the Hydra's poison from Heracles' arrow. Nessus's advice to Deianeira that the blood be used as a love potion is uncannily right. The Centaur dies

because of his own lust, and his revenge can only be fulfilled when
Deianeira is driven by Heracles' lust to use it. Heracles is killed by
his own poison and by his likeness to his own victim.

This exchange of the past is the vehicle for the gift-exchange of
Heracles and Deianeira. The sending of Iole and the return of the
poisoned robe are parodies of an exchange between the riches of
the outer world and those of the house. The irony is embedded in
the role of Lichas, who is promised (618) a twofold gratitude from
herself and Heracles if he acts as a faithful messenger. This thanks,
charis, is the central word in the ethics of exchange; it characterizes
both giver and recipient. Lichas has tried to be kind, and so been
unfaithful to both Deianeira and Heracles. He has brought one gift
for which no thanks are due, and he is about to bring another.
Deianeira bitterly calls Iole an *oikouria,* a repayment for her house-
keeping (542). She tells Lichas she wants him to bring "gifts as
fitting return for gifts" (493–96), for it is improper that one who
brought so much should go back empty-handed. It is unclear whether
in these lines Deianeira is already planning the sending of the robe,
which she explains in the next scene, or whether her words show a
naive desire to behave correctly.

Later she says that the gift of a new robe fulfills a vow she had
made (613), as the sacrifices at which Heracles is to wear the garment
fulfill his promise to the gods (240). So the idea of sending it is
probably independent of the anointing, which renders it "newer"
than it was and "newer" than Deianeira knows. The robe is sent
first as a direct expression of mutual affection, and then as an attempt
to create a reciprocity of feeling. Hence in her message she hesitates
to say how she longs for Heracles "before I know if I am longed for
there" (632). But the only reciprocities which function here are
those of cruelty and death. Iole and the robe are matching offerings,
and Heracles will seek to kill Deianeira so that "she may tell everyone
that Heracles requited evildoers" (1111). All response is hostile.

Lies and Causes

Much of the factual background of the action is given in the false
speech of Lichas (248–90), where it has been subject to compression
and distortion. Some of its information is duplicated. Heracles'
slavery to Omphale is known to Hyllus in the prologue, and serves
to prepare for the inversion of sexual roles late in the play, when

Heracles will cry out like a woman (1075) and Deianeira will kill herself with the male weapon, the sword. Deianeira knows of the murder of Iphitus, which has led to the family's exile (38); it may be typical of her life with Heracles that she does not seem to know of Heracles' punishment for that crime, but her knowledge does confirm Lichas's description of the murder and its connection with Heracles' enslavement. According to Lichas, Zeus would have forgiven Heracles had he killed Iphitus in fair fight, since "the gods do not love outrage any more than men" (280). The outrage is presumably that offered Heracles when he visited Eurytus (262–69):

Who . . . insulted him greatly, with a mad heart, saying that even with inescapable arrows he was inferior to Eurytus' sons as an archer, and calling him the broken slave of a free man. And at dinner, when Heracles was drunk, he threw him outdoors.

The chain of events given here—insults, murder of Iphitus, enslavement of Heracles, is presumably the "slight complaint" (361) Heracles used to justify his war. Though this tale is a pretext, it is not thereby a lie, and its ingredients are traditional. But it is hard to reconcile this sequence with the role of Iole. According to one version, Eurytus offered Iole in marriage to anyone who could defeat his sons and himself in archery, but denied her to the victorious Heracles; the reference to archery seems like an allusion to a form of this story, but a confused one (did Eurytus cheat?). Heracles is called a slave because of his famous labors, but these have ended by this point, unless this insult long precedes Heracles' vengeance. It seems that details of different legends have been mixed together so that each part has the ring of familiar, and hence true material, but the whole does not cohere.[8] Lichas does not lie, only omits—but the crucial facts cannot simply be fitted into his account. What we are told is necessary to understanding the series of events, yet we do not know how Heracles fell in love and was refused.

So there is a double causal nexus, with an elaborate causal chain that serves as foil for the real, but obscure cause, *eros*. This explanation makes other causes irrelevant. The deceit is more than foil, however. It prepares us for the credulity of Deianeira in accepting Nessus's gift by showing her caught in a world where truth and deceit are closely joined. And it adds a further reciprocity: Heracles, like Ajax, left his nature and killed through guile, and so, in a sense, made himself vulnerable to his own death by guile. The deceit of concealment practiced by Lichas is the deceit Deianeira attempts in her secret use of the charm. Craft is a woman's weapon (so Heracles' craft results in subordination to women), but it is not in Deianeira's nature. She tells Lichas (453–54): "It is an evil fate for a free man to be called a liar." She is evidently embarrassed by the subterfuge of the robe.[9] Nonetheless, she does try to use craft. Her error is double. She acts on insufficient evidence, and learns the truth too late; the pervasive secrecy of the play marks a world where to act without full knowledge is dangerous, yet knowledge is almost impossible to obtain.[10] But she also, to a small degree, tries to imitate the deceit of the world in which she lives; as Nessus's lust is echoed in Heracles, his falsehood is echoed in her.

Oracles

The epistemological problem is manifest in the oracles. An oracle represents absolute truth, and in this play the chief oracle is in written form, and so should not be subject to distortion. Yet thematically the oracles resemble Nessus's promise that Heracles would love no woman more than his wife. The words are a riddle and a prophecy (Nessus, dying, has a special access to truth).[11] The gift of Nessus, like the oracle, is "old" (555), and Deianeira remembers the instructions as perfectly as if she had written them in bronze (683). The bewildering message has a stable shape, in which it survives from an artificially remote past.

The oracle is first named as merely a writing-tablet (47–48). A few lines later we hear that Heracles will die or live happily after a struggle in Euboea. Then Deianeira tells the chorus that her husband left her an "ancient" tablet, saying that at the end of fifteen months he would die or live untroubled, according to Zeus's oracle at Dodona. So the oracle has apparently shifted from specifying a place to signaling a time. When the messenger announces Heracles' victory, the oracle is ignored. Psychologically, this neglect may be referred to a natural assumption on Deianeira's part that the victory means the oracle is fulfilled, but it is notable that for Deianeira to act the oracle must be ignored, not misunderstood. At 647–49 the chorus says that Heracles has been gone a year rather than fifteen months. This could be a mere slip, but at 821–30 the oracle has a different time limit, no longer fifteen months from Heracles' departure but twelve years from the giving of the oracle. While this is not a contradiction, the restatement seems to press a curious symmetry: the twelve-month absence ends a twelve-year period. At the same time, the antiquity of this twelve-year-old oracle is stressed. Time is both expanded, so that twelve years is an age, and contracted, so that the implied expanses of time lead only to the moment at which the oracle is fulfilled. Moreover, the oracle no longer has alternatives. Now the chorus says that the oracle promised Heracles release from his labors; the maidens, knowing how he has been struck by the poison, interpret this release as his death. When Hyllus tells his father of Nessus's role, Heracles immediately realizes that death is imminent, since Zeus told him "long ago" he would be killed by an inhabitant of the nether world; this prophecy is congruent with those he wrote down at Dodona, where Zeus said he would be freed from labor at the time which is now present. The oracles which were old are now new compared to a yet older oracle. Thus the oracle from Dodona shifts continually: it referred to place or to time, it was recent or ancient, it presented an alternative or an ambiguity.

This last change is important and the minor inconsistencies are probably present in order to emphasize it. The earlier version is not merely another statement of the later, ambiguous wording, for the word "life" appears in one of the possible outcomes both times it is cited. The first version could be an interpretation of the second, giving its two possible meanings as real alternatives. It is never possible to tell whether an oracle which offers alternatives (whether explicitly or through ambiguity) really means that different outcomes are possible, depending on human action, or whether the gods simply refuse to be too precise. For mortals this distinction is irrelevant, since they must act as if their actions could affect outcomes. This is a clue to the oracle. The first version is given by Deianeira, before the event. The second comes from the chorus as the girls consider Heracles' fate and from Heracles himself, after the donning of the fatal robe. For her the gods have decreed an action which causes Heracles' death, while for him there is a pattern discerned after the fact, a fulfillment of destiny. There is only one oracle from Dodona, and the varying versions are not different interpretations; rather even a message from the gods is subjective, differing according to the recipient and his situation. If the oracle prophesied death all along, Deianeira's act would lose in moral meaning; if it did not, the death of Heracles would be accidental, not the essential end of Zeus's dark intention. Even an absolute truth preserved in immutable form is fluid; yet the oracles also confirm the results of causes far removed in time. Heracles' misunderstanding of the release from labor parallels Deianeira's misunderstanding of Nessus's gift, while he comprehends simultaneously two oracles, that of death from one no longer alive and that of release from labor. This congruence of oracles marks a congruence of causes: the actions of the protagonists mesh to fulfill both the will of Nessus and the will of Zeus.

Gods

Aphrodite and Eros.   The tragedy is the work of Aphrodite and her associate Eros, the deities of sexual passion. These are powers beyond human control, yet they work through mortals. The central section of the drama is, in effect, a study in the working of sexual love. When Deianeira learns why her husband has sacked Oechalia, she explains that she cannot blame him for being conquered by Eros since she knows (443–44) that he "rules any of the gods he wishes/ and myself: so how not another like me?" The following choral ode demonstrates the power of Aphrodite, "who always carries off a mighty victory" (497) by hinting at the many loves of Zeus and then recalling the battle of Heracles and Achelous, where Aphrodite was umpire. This song points in many directions: Heracles' many amours seem an imitation of his divine father's, while his very existence is the result of rampant *eros*. Deianeira is both subject to passion, as she admits, and the victim of the passions of others. Love is associated with struggle and combat, and Deianeira had feared long ago (25) that her beauty might prove a grief to her; now it is Iole's beauty which has destroyed her city. Iole has been an object of combat; yet the song establishes the norm of sexual rivalry, and so prepares for a contest between Deianeira and Iole for Heracles.

Deianeira's attitude toward her husband and her rival is remarkably generous and shows *sophrosyne*—Eros is a god, with whom she knows better than to fight. Yet her very excuse for Heracles gives her no defense against her own erotic impulse. In the past, she forgave Heracles' liaisons (459–62). But now she is growing older, and moreover Iole has been sent to Deianeira's home, where the two will lie "under one blanket" (539–40). Heracles will be Deianeira's spouse, but the other's lover (547–51). Deianeira cannot endure the complete loss of her husband. When she uses love's power over herself to excuse others she does not recognize the destructive strength of that power; or the admission itself may increase her subjection to *eros*. In any case, like cunning, *eros* seems to require a suitable medium to work its havoc: Deianeira's *eros* transmits the blood of Nessus to Heracles.

At least two recurrent images, heat and disease, link *eros* with the poison of Nessus.[12] The sexless world of virgins is a shelter to which the sun's heat does not penetrate (145). Heracles is "hot" with love for Iole (368), and she is "melted" with desire for him (463). The poison must be kept in darkness, and begins to work when exposed to sunlight and the heat of sacrificial fire. It melts away the bit of wool when the sun strikes it, and Heracles is seen as "fused" with the charm of the robe (662—this passage, however, is textually uncertain). The poison is activated by heat, as if by *eros* itself. And *eros* is a disease (445, 544). This metaphorical disease causes the disease of the poison (1013, 1115, 1120). The deaths of both protagonists are erotic, Heracles' through the melting and hot closeness of the poison (he is "melted against the terrible image of the Hydra" at 836), and Deianeira's in her opening of her clothing as she sits on her marriage-bed and plunges in the sword. "The attendant Aphrodite, though silent, has appeared as the evident accomplisher of this," sings the chorus at 859–60.

Zeus. Aphrodite, whether seen as an independent divinity or as a projection of human drives, is not expected to be other than irrational and destructive. But Zeus is supreme among the gods, and justice is in his keeping. He is also the father of Heracles. Zeus is constantly present in the play, beginning with the entry-song of the chorus, which reminds Deianeira that Zeus has not made mortal life painless, but changeable; yet he cannot be unmindful of his children (126–30, 139–40). Zeus is the lord of nearby Mt. Oeta, it is he who required Heracles' service to Omphale, he who gave the oracles. And in the final lines, he is called the author of all that has taken place (1275–78). While such a statement, which indicts the god for allowing events to follow their natural course, cannot represent a complete understanding, there must be a special reason for such a bitter summary at the close. Heracles himself seems to accuse Zeus of failing in *charis,* a fair return for the sacrifices during which the poison struck (993–95): the rules of reciprocity, which he was piously following, were ignored by the god. Zeus is not required to explain events; only the servitude to Omphale and perhaps the success of the expedition against Oechalia are actually his doing. But Heracles' life has been lived under the eye of Zeus, with its endless labor and fighting against monsters. The characters expect and demand his help, even to demanding a miracle, and the spectator is easily drawn into their expectation.

To attribute events to Zeus is to insist that they conform to a rational plan, obscure though it be. But this design may be no more than the rules he has set down for mortal life, which allow no one to escape without suffering. In the *Iliad,* Heracles is the example of a universal rule: even Heracles dies (18. 117). That he permits even his own son to suffer and die may prove only that gods are unlike mortals. Yet the oracles do suggest a pattern unique to Heracles, some particular concern which is hidden under the visible causal chain. And this leads to the question of Heracles' apotheosis.[13] By the mid-fifth century, the common version of the myth had Heracles ascend to Mt. Olympus, to live happily as a god, and this ascent was, at least sometimes, imagined as taking place from the pyre on Mt. Oeta. The play makes no direct allusion to this myth, but details of the conclusion seem to hint at it. Heracles insists that the pyre will end his suffering. It is to be built of oak and olive, used in the cult of Heracles on Mt. Oeta. Hyllus will build but not light it (this was done by Philoctetes or his father Poeas). The very fact that the pyre is so emphasized would have brought the myth to the minds of the audience.

Nonetheless, there is no clear sign, and Heracles expects nothing but death. He threatens Hyllus that if his son disobeys him, he will be a curse on Hyllus from below (1201–02). Yet the tone changes drastically when Heracles realizes that the oracles are fulfilled and his death is near. Though Hyllus speaks in order to exonerate his mother, Heracles has no interest in her. He has final arrangements to make, and asks for his mother and other children, resting content with Hyllus when he learns that the rest of the family is far away. His lamentations end. Instead his tone becomes peremptory as he demands that Hyllus prepare the pyre without tears. There is no mark of any special understanding, except that the oracles are fulfilled. Heracles has a very particular knowledge of how his death must come about, but not why. When he has obtained Hyllus's consent to the building of his pyre, he demands a second "slight favor" *(charis),* that Hyllus marry Iole. No other man is to have the woman who once lay by him (1225–26). Hyllus's reaction is horrified; not only is the connection almost incestuous, but the girl has been partly responsible for the deaths of both his parents. But Heracles insists. Heracles does not seem to be concerned for either the girl or his son, but neither does his insistence merely show his egoism. In mythological tradition, Hyllus and Iole were ancestors of a line of kings. Sophocles was under no compulsion to introduce this future into the drama, nor does Heracles appear to know of it, but the audience surely remembered it.

Clearly the two demands of Heracles are closely related. In each case he insists on apparently dreadful acts which actually lead to blessings: his own ascent to heaven, his son's foundation of a dynasty. Yet he does not seem to know what he is doing. Rather he shows yet again the prophetic quality of the dying: his fierce will is in complete harmony with divine will. This is more than a bow to mythological tradition on the poet's part; rather that mythological history, which fulfills the will of Zeus, speaks through a Heracles who is ignorant of it. The strange conjunction gives the close its curious power. The oracle will in the end be fulfilled even beyond Heracles' last interpretation of it, for Heracles' unique destiny unites its irreconcilable formulations. In dying on the pyre and then becoming a god on Olympus, Heracles will both die and live without care.

But this happy future is imposed on the characters, who are not allowed to see it. Moreover, Zeus's ultimate design is no clearer in the larger history of which the play's action is a part than in the play itself. There is no hint as to why this future required so much suffering, and Deianeira is granted no consolation. Indeed, while Heracles himself may be granted eternal happiness, Hyllus and his siblings still have many troubles before them—troubles foreshadowed in the prayer of Deianeira that she not live to see her children suffer like the captives from Oechalia (304–5). Heracles' declaration of imperatives he himself does not understand underscores the theme of Deianeira's choice: even when the dying hero announces purposes shared by himself and Zeus, he does not know Zeus's design. We can see more of that design from our later historical position, but our own world is as dark to us as that of the characters in the drama is to them. A wider purpose in apparently senseless human affairs is the concern of Zeus, but that pattern is invisible within the human world. This truth is not presented as a moralizing lesson to show that mortals should be humble because they lack divine omniscience, nor is it an attack on the gods, whose grand designs, examined in detail, are woven of such pathos. The play strikes an uneasy balance. On one side is the vision of Zeus and the mythological history we know, on the other the world of human choices and limits. At the end of the play, we are presented with the point at which they intersect most bluntly. As long as Heracles lives, he lives in ignorance.

Chapter Four

The Causes of Ruin: *Antigone*

Background and Plot

Antigone concerns family ties in opposition to political demands, and it assumes knowledge of a complex mythological history. Oedipus in ignorance married his mother, Jocasta, and the couple had four children: Antigone, Ismene, Eteocles, and Polynices. When Oedipus's parricide and incest were revealed, Jocasta hanged herself; there were varying stories about the fate of Oedipus, but in the version used in *Antigone,* he apparently died at Thebes, where the play is set. His two sons then quarreled over the kingship; Polynices, driven into exile, gathered an army in alliance with Argos and attacked his native city. The Argives were defeated, and the brothers killed each other. Creon, Jocasta's brother, became king. A chart may help:

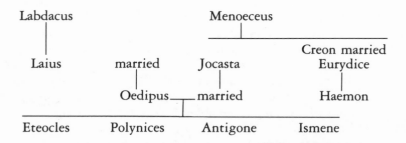

Labdacus   Menoeceus

Laius   married   Jocasta   Creon married Eurydice

Oedipus —— married   Haemon

Eteocles   Polynices   Antigone   Ismene

The play opens before dawn, as Antigone summons Ismene outside to tell her the news. Creon, the new ruler, has ordered that Eteocles is to be buried with due rites, while Polynices is to be left unburied, as a traitor. Antigone seeks the help of her sister in defying the edict. Ismene cannot help. She is a woman, not fit to fight with men, and she will not oppose the city. The rest of the family has already perished miserably, and Antigone's folly can bring only more misery. Antigone, on the other hand, says simply that Creon has

43

no right to interfere with her familial obligations. The dead man is her brother, and the gods honor the burial ritual. There is a longer time to spend among the dead than the living, and they must rather be pleased. Ismene offers to keep Antigone's act secret; Antigone bids her rather proclaim it. As she exits, Ismene calls her "foolish, but to thy dear ones truly dear" (99).[1]

The chorus enters, singing a hymn to the rising sun, who has put the enemy army to flight. One captain's fate is especially mentioned, Capaneus, who for his boasting was struck by Zeus's thunderbolt as he was about to set fire to the ramparts. All is Theban triumph, except the mutual slaughter of the two brothers. Now Dionysus should rule a joyous Thebes. Creon enters (155) to promulgate his edict to the elders of the chorus. First he states his principles, that the ruler must keep to the best advice, undeterred by fear, and must prefer civic interest to every other. Hence Polynices, who would have destroyed his own city, shall be left unburied as carrion. The chorus responds that the edict is within Creon's power. But one of the watchmen set over the corpse by the king now enters (223) to report that the body has been buried: the first watchman of the day found it lightly covered with dust. No tools were used, no animal has come near. Creon, certain that the guard has been bribed by his political rivals, warns him with threats to find the doer. When the chorus hints that perhaps the gods were involved, Creon angrily insists that they would not care for one who tried to burn their shrines. The guard leaves in fear, while the chorus sings of human achievement: "Awesome things are many, but none more awesome than man." He has developed seafaring and agriculture, he traps and tames wild animals, has gained speech and thought, and medicine; yet his skills lead sometimes to good, sometimes to evil. As long as he upholds law, his city is high, but wrong and recklessness make him cityless.[2]

The guard enters with Antigone (384). Having uncovered the body, the guards watched until midday, when a dust-storm forced them to close their eyes. When the whirlwind quieted, they saw Antigone lamenting, scattering dust, and pouring libations. Antigone, questioned, is defiant. Creon has no power to override the justice of the gods below and the divine unwritten ordinances. Nor does she see death as an evil. Creon responds that her relationship to himself will not save her; if she defeats him, she is the man, not he. When he argues that one brother would have opposed burying the other, she says she was born to join in love, not hate (523). Ismene is brought in, and claims to have shared the deed—if Antigone agrees. But she does not. Ismene asks whether Creon will kill his son's betrothed; Creon replies that other women are available. The sisters are taken indoors. The chorus sings of the curse on such houses as that of Labdacus, where a divine power urges the race to ruin. The last light here has been cut down by a "folly of speech, a Fury [an avenging goddess] in the mind" (600–603). Evil seems good to one whom a god leads to ruin, and nothing great enters mortal life without disaster.

Haemon, Creon's son, enters, declaring his filial loyalty. Creon, praising obedience, urges him to "spit out" Antigone. But Haemon claims that the citizens support her, and Creon should yield. Creon accuses his son of being a woman's slave, while Haemon claims to speak in concern for his father and the gods. Haemon leaves in rage (765), and Creon (accepting the chorus's advice to spare Ismene) decrees that Antigone will be entombed in a lonely vault with enough food that the city will escape the pollution of killing her.[3] The chorus sings a hymn to unconquerable Eros, causer of this family quarrel. Antigone, brought in under guard, sings a lament in responsion with the chorus (806–82). She stresses the strangeness of her fate, which places her among neither the living nor the dead, and the sorrow of dying without marriage or children. In her last speech, she addresses her tomb/bridal chamber, and expects her family's welcome below; she prays that if her enemies are wrong, they suffer nothing worse than what they are doing to her. She is led off (943), and the chorus runs through various mythological precedents: Danae was locked away by her father, though she bore the son of Zeus; King Lycurgus, opponent of Dionysus, was imprisoned, and Cleopatra, though descended from gods, endured the blinding of her sons by their stepmother.[4] At song's end, the blind prophet Tiresias enters (988) to tell Creon that his communication with the gods has been cut off by the pollution spread by the birds who have feasted on human flesh. When Creon insults the prophet, claiming he has been bribed, Tiresias answers that Creon, who has buried the living while exposing the dead, will pay with his own family, and leaves. Creon is frightened, consults the chorus, and changes his mind. The chorus sings for the Theban god Dionysus to purify the city.

A messenger enters (1155) and reports to the chorus and Creon's wife, Eurydice. Creon buried the remains of Polynices and went to the tomb. Antigone had hanged herself. Haemon had broken in. He spat on his father, tried to kill him with his sword, and then plunged the sword into himself. Eurydice in silence goes into the house. Creon enters with Haemon's body (1257), lamenting his own folly, and a messenger from within briefly reports that Eurydice has killed herself. The doors are opened to reveal her, and the drama ends as Creon, broken and wishing for death, goes indoors.

The Central Conflict

This is an easily approachable, though not an easy work. Its basic dramatic conflict involves two characters and two principles: Creon embodies the state and its authority, Antigone the family and its religious tradition. This conflict is expressed in two closely related issues, Creon's refusal of burial to Polynices and Antigone's refusal to obey his edict. There is no doubt which side is in the right. Our sympathy is with Antigone from the start, and by the end the gods have visibly proved her right. But to emphasize merely the rightness of Antigone and the folly of Creon is to sentimentalize a work that is in no way sentimental. The complexity of the play does not reside in any fair balance of moral right and wrong between the opposing sides. Rather the central conflict is only one element in a drama which explores, as much as any of Sophocles' tragedies, the ambiguities of divine will and human action, of reason and irrationality. The moral of the play is not that the dead should be buried; but the dispute over the burial is the motive force and the framework.

Polynices' crime, the attempt to sack his native city, is one of the worst imaginable for a Greek, and in the entry-song of the chorus the horror of his attack is vivid. He is a bloodthirsty eagle. Even Antigone never defends him. In Athenian law, a traitor could not be buried in Attic soil. The relatives of one executed for treason could, however, carry his body beyond the border and give it funeral rites. [5] Creon's edict thus transgresses ordinary practice. Yet the final outcome also violates normal rules in that Polynices is buried within the borders of Thebes. Moreover, Greek literature reveals complex attitudes to the rule that the dead must receive proper burial. While the *Iliad* ends with the episode of reconciliation in which Achilles, at divine urging, restores the body of his enemy Hector to his family for burial, Menelaus would have exposed the body of his brother's murderer had he been able,[6] although in the epic Menelaus is a sympathetic character.

Antigone's claim is double. On the one hand, she asserts the simple right of the family and the claims of affection: her duty to bury a brother is a matter with which no one has a right to interfere. At the same time, she defends her act as demanded by "unwritten ordinances" (450–55):

> It was not Zeus who proclaimed this, nor does Justice who lives with the gods below establish such laws among men. I did not think your edicts were so strong that as a mortal you could override the secure, unwritten usages of the gods.

"Unwritten laws" appear to have been a topic of controversy in the second half of the fifth century.[7] Thucydides has Pericles in the Funeral Oration speak of Athenian obedience to those laws "which, though unwritten, confer an acknowledged shame" (2.37.3), while an orator quotes Pericles as using the term for a ritual law ([Lysias] 6.9). Xenophon shows Socrates and the sophist Hippias discussing unwritten, universal laws such as those which enjoin gratitude to benefactors or forbid incest and demand reverence for the gods.[8] These laws are attributed to the gods, and serve as a bridge between *physis,* nature, and *nomos,* custom, which anthropological study and speculation had sharply divided. Antigone's appeal is probably not based on a recognized inclusion of the duty to bury the dead as an unwritten law. But it was a traditional obligation to offer at least symbolic burial to an exposed body; the guard compares the first burial to the dust thrown by a wayfarer who offers it to avoid a curse (256). Such an obligation could easily be put among "unwritten laws" as a basic act of piety, and its definition as such a law has great emotional power. Linked in the figure of Antigone with the equally basic law of devotion to family, her claim persuasively evokes fundamental responses. An unburied corpse violates the natural and religious order, for the dead belong beneath the earth. A sister who protects her brother is to be admired (since he no longer threatens the community). The appeal to the unwritten ordinances is original, but convincing and moving.

The speech raises a fundamental problem of which Antigone is not necessarily aware. She is concerned for the immediate issue, and knows only that eternal, divine law supersedes human law just as it is more important to please the dead than the living. Her speech, however, has been preceded in the play by Creon's discussion of political principles and by the chorus's view of human progress in the "Ode on Man." The ode has celebrated mortal development. Man "taught himself" language, thought, civic life.[9] Antigone appeals to rules whose origin is unknown (456). Creon rightly says that only within the city can we make friends; individual life depends on the common good. Yet Antigone's devotion is to those "friends" whom we do not make for ourselves (Her act and her claim are a reminder that the city is formed of families, that human life is not a matter of pure choice; they continue the pondering of the chorus on the unsure direction of progress. "While he honors the law of the land and sworn justice of the gods, high is his city" (369–70). No one doubts that well-being depends on reverence toward the gods and justice. But for Creon the city is the basis for judging justice and piety; the chorus is ambiguous; Antigone asserts that there is another standard, but she does not refer to any public, civic standard. If Antigone is right, her very refusal to consider civic interest is the position which benefits the city, and in the end she is proved right.

Her rightness, however, solves only the particular question and leaves the wider question open. Creon is put decisively in the wrong by his unwillingness to listen to good advice: the chorus which suggests divine concern, Haemon who warns of popular opinion, and Tiresias with his prophetic message. He also, in burying Antigone alive, repeats his violation of eternal law in a clearer form, inverting the proper places of living and dead. But the true relation of the different spheres is unresolved: the city, a human creation, but one whose survival is the basis of civilized life, and whose survival depends on obedience to its laws; the families who constitute the city and can yet conflict with it; the gods whose requirements are eternal, yet unwritten, and thus not codified or clear.

Antigone

Ismene. Antigone is entirely right, and there are obvious problems in presenting a heroine whose actions embody justice. But this is not a story of innocent suffering or simple martyrdom. Antigone is not vindicated until late in the action, though she always has our sympathies. These, however, cannot be one-sided. Antigone is balanced against other characters and against wider forces. The most obvious foil character is Ismene, whose timidity defines Antigone's courage. Like Odysseus in the prologue of *Ajax,* she is a vehicle for turning audience sensibility: she believes that Antigone is right to insist that the burial is just, but considers Antigone foolish in attempting the impossible and exceeding a woman's position.

But the debate shows an Antigone whose loyalty to family can quickly become rejection. She uses terms of actual hatred to her sister (86, 93). Her very refusal to acknowledge the mutual hatred so prominent in her family—she insists on equal care for brothers who killed each other—expresses itself in a division with her living sister. Her kindness to the dead is not matched in kindness to the living. Yet Ismene's last words in the prologue show her as still loving her sister. (Antigone can be loved even by the sister whose love she rejects, while Ismene's lack of greatness allows a generosity her sister lacks.) And when we next hear of Ismene, she is described as hysterical: Creon thinks this is a sign of guilt, but we recognize her pain and fear (488–92).

When she reappears (526), the conflict becomes more intense, for she now seeks to equal Antigone in what only shortly before she called "folly" and is folly to Creon now (562). Ismene has now, in effect, accepted Antigone's view. She asks what life is left for her, if her sister dies (548), just as Antigone had insisted that she did not object to death since her family had suffered so much. Yet Antigone replies (549) by telling her to ask Creon; she calls her sister "A friend who loves in words," as if a desire to share her death were not deed enough. Antigone performed her act alone, and she refuses to allow Ismene any share in it. Yet at 553 she becomes slightly more gentle: "Save yourself. I do not begrudge your escape." The line introduces an ambiguity into Antigone's motives: she rejects Ismene both out of justice, for she cannot allow her to share the credit for what she did not do, and because she does not wish her death. In her last words to Ismene (559–60), she sums up the difference in nature between them: "Have courage. You live, but my soul long ago / Died, so as to help the dead." Ismene can try to sacrifice herself for Antigone, but only an Antigone, already in some sense devoted, will sacrifice herself for the dead. [10]

Ismene is concerned with the affections of life, and appropriately it is she who protests Creon's killing of his son's betrothed. As Antigone presses austerely on to death, Ismene links her with the world of the living. After her exit at 581, Ismene is mentioned only once. Haemon, the lover Ismene has first named, in the following scene provides a further connection between Antigone and the living world. And the final Antigone, who can lament her fate, has absorbed something of both her supporters. Ismene has fulfilled her function, humanizing her sister even when she seems least humane, and suggesting that actions like Antigone's are not merely the result of goodwill.

Haemon.   Haemon's love for Antigone is an important factor in the action, as the mechanism by which Creon's error returns against himself. But the two never meet on stage, and we see them together only in the messenger's speech describing the terrible events at the tomb. Antigone only once (even if she speaks 572) mentions him;[11] that their love is mutual is certain only from Ismene's single remark at 570, when she answers Creon's claim that Haemon can produce his heir elsewhere—"The fields of others can be ploughed too"—with "But not as suited as for him and for her." Antigone dies in utter isolation; Haemon can join her only by joining in her death, as Ismene sought to do. Yet her love for him, though barely mentioned, is like her hint of concern for Ismene's survival: some attachment to the living is still present in the death-devoted maiden of the first part of the play.

The episode between Creon and Haemon is introduced by a choral announcement (626–30). The chorus's question—does he come in grief at the loss of his bride?—defines *eros* as the theme of the scene. But when Creon in effect repeats this question, Haemon declares that no marriage means more to him than his father. Creon praises obedience. Not only should Haemon obey his father, but he should recognize that Antigone's disobedience proves her a bad woman and hence unattractive, "a cold embrace" (650). Haemon speaks in purely rational terms, as one concerned only for his father's best interest. But Creon refuses to believe that his son has any motive but passion. When Haemon cries that Antigone's death will lead to another's (751), it is clearly the lover who speaks. Yet Haemon is no hypocrite. Creon is apparently incapable of accepting the complexity of human motives, or of listening seriously to an argument which is made because the speaker is in love. For him, Haemon cannot love both Antigone and himself, or say something true for emotional reasons.

Haemon is a subsidiary character, but this episode reveals a complexity which is reiterated in the scene at the tomb. His love and his filial piety are in ultimate conflict. Although he threatened suicide earlier, his death is not directly motivated by grief for Antigone, but by anger at himself after his attack on his father, according to the messenger (1235–36). The disaster for Creon requires that Haemon's loyalty to him be strong enough to cause his destructive and instant remorse.

At the same time, the final image of the dead lovers lying side by side is explicitly erotic: this death is the consummation of a marriage (1240–41). Antigone in the second half of the play has lamented both in song and in spoken verse her virgin death. Her burial alive is a kind of living descent into the netherworld, where she will become the bride of Death. Her laments point two ways. On the one hand, her regret at dying without marriage or children affirms what the figures of Ismene and Haemon have suggested, that despite her apparent devotion to death, she is not without attachments in life: she has not sacrificed a life which had no worth. She too is a complex person. And despite Creon's fear that she seeks to usurp a male role, her lament echoes her concern with funeral ritual, an especially female role—what she misses is the normal woman's life. At the same time, she does not name her betrothed and sees herself as dying unlamented, though the audience has seen Ismene's love for her—Ismene she has rejected, and she never learns of Haemon's fidelity. On the other hand, her agony can be linked to a sense that the entombment does not simply join her with the dead (850–51)—she will belong to neither world. Antigone was able to abandon life in order to be united with the dead, but her peculiar fate deprives her even of this. Deeply drawn to both worlds, she is deprived of both. When, in her last speech, she speaks of her hope that she will be a dear arrival to her family (897–99), suicide may already be on her mind.

   Creon. The tragedy ends with the laments of Creon, and his fate in some ways conforms better to a popular idea of tragedy. He is ruined through his own mistakes, though the punishment is excessive in proportion to the crime; he learns wisdom through suffering, and too late. Creon's fate is an object lesson, a moral tale;

and in this way he is a brilliant foil to the central figure, Antigone, whose fate is caused by greater forces and is more ambiguous.

Creon makes two basic errors, which appear in all he does. First, he cannot apply his excellent rules to anyone but himself. He stresses the need to hold to the best plans and to speak the truth without fear, but we hear that the citizens are afraid to tell him what they think, and he rejects good advice from Haemon and the chorus. Condemning Antigone's loyalty to family ties, he expects absolute loyalty from Haemon (634). He is obsessed with social definitions: the king should rule, the son obey, women be subordinate. Thus he applies one rule to each entity. He first receives advice when the prophet frightens him. At last he turns to the chorus to ask what he should do (1099). This moment at which he changes his mind unites two sudden recognitions—that others can be right as well as himself and that he too values his family, and so is vulnerable.

His second error is more interesting. The hierarchical world he imagines he lives in is also a rational world. The family, in his speech to Haemon, is a small model of the city, and the city and the army are analogous. People have only one motive for any action: Haemon is in love, and therefore his arguments can be disregarded. He assumes that anyone who would bury Polynices must be a political enemy, and that the guard was bribed. Later in the play, after he knows of Antigone's burial of Polynices, he can still accuse Tiresias of having been bribed. Money and power, "rational" goals, are what he understands, and any opposition to him must be the work either of those seeking to depose him or of victims of madness.

This overrationality applies also to the gods, where it is most dangerous. Creon is by no means impious; his opening words piously attribute the salvation of the city to the gods. But he assumes that the gods, whose concern for the city has been thus proved, reason as he does himself. Surely they cannot care for Polynices, who tried to burn their shrines (284–89). The gods do not honor the wicked. He is confident that his distinctions are also theirs. Again, when Tiresias reports that the gods, offended by the carrion which pollutes their altars, refuse to accept his sacrifices, he insists that mortals cannot pollute the gods, even if the birds bring carrion to the throne of Zeus (1040–44). That the gods could not be polluted was not a new or impious belief, though most people probably assumed otherwise. But he draws an overprecise conclusion: if the gods are not polluted by an unburied corpse, his refusal to bury Polynices cannot offend them. He does fear ritual pollution, and has Antigone entombed with a little food so that the city will avoid a curse in her death (773–76). This is a technical evasion, normal in Greek religious thinking. But in burying Antigone alive he repeats the offense against divine and natural order he committed in denying burial to Polynices. He thinks legally and logically, but the gods seem to be allied rather with the simple human feeling which is repelled by an unburied corpse, carrion on an altar of the gods, or burial alive.

Appropriately, Creon is destroyed by his son's emotional conflict and his wife's grief and anger. His own family is governed by the basic emotions he has denied, and he is vulnerable because he also is human and loves his wife and son. Chance or the gods keep him from reaching the tomb in time; the world does not allow each intention to attain a fixed and matching result. Creon is forced to recognize the power of the irrational, and he admits his guilt in the deaths of Haemon and Eurydice. He is pathetic and demands sympathy, as he reveals how ruinous human folly can be. The chorus has claimed that "nothing great comes into the life of mortals without ruin" (613–14). Creon has met forces beyond his power.

The Curse

Creon is not by nature akin to this accursed greatness, but Antigone is. The chorus delivers this claim in contemplating Antigone's clan, the Labdacids. For the chorus, Antigone's self-destructive act is merely the last in a long line of divinely ordained troubles: "Whose house is shaken by a god, nothing of disaster is omitted" (584– 85). The singers identify the curse with Antigone's *physis,* the nature she has inherited from her ancestors; she is the victim of "a bloody dust belonging to the nether gods, a folly of speech and a Fury in the mind" (601–3). [12] The elders call her "violent child of a violent father" (471). The curse is an external reality, but works within Antigone herself. In the prologue, Ismene presented the griefs of the house as a reason for self-restraint, while for Antigone they are a reason to desire death. Her devotion to her family is inevitably a devotion to death, not only because so many have died, but because ruin and self-destruction are their characteristics.

The chorus joins thoughts of the curse with condemnation of Antigone in their Aeschylean lament (853–56):

Advancing to the farthest point of daring, you have had a great fall against the high throne of Justice: but you are expiating some ancestral ordeal.

Although Antigone has committed no injustice, it is not the accusation to which she responds in her part of the lament. Instead she laments her birth from an incestuous marriage and her brother's ill-fated wedding with an Argive princess. She calls herself a "curse-bearer" (867); she fulfills the curse in herself and also spreads it to Creon's family. The chorus is clearly right in seeing the curse at work in the play. It would be a mistake, however, to modernize the curse into a mere familial capacity for self-destruction: the curse works both through Antigone and Creon and in the situation itself. Moreover, Antigone's action is morally right and demanded by the gods, even as it embodies their curse; and no offense of the Labdacids against the gods is cited to justify divine hatred. [13]

Within the plain contest of right and wrong is a complex network of causality and of involved sympathy. We cannot but feel sympathetic understanding for Ismene, whom Antigone rejects. Antigone acts rightly, yet is driven by a curse. In the first part of the play she desires death, but her laments reveal her regret for life, for marriage and children. Creon is wrong, but he is not merely stupid, obstinate, or impious. He cannot believe that the gods defend their own enemies. Haemon cannot reconcile his sense of duty to his father with his anger at him or his love for Antigone.

Much of the choral moralizing in this play is highly ambiguous. The song about the curse of the Labdacids ends with a reminder of the awesome power of Zeus and the deception of human expectation. The victim of hope perceives nothing until his foot is in the fire (620–25):

Wisely did the famous saying appear, that evil seems good at some time to him whose mind a god leads to ruin. He is outside ruin only briefly.

The chorus has Antigone in mind, of course, and a god is indeed leading her to destruction. Yet the following scene is that between Creon and Haemon, and they too are on their way to destruction. Haemon is maddened by Eros according to the chorus (790); Creon is insane according to his son (765). And a god cooperates in their madness.

The Gods and the Two Burials

The gods do not intervene blatantly in the action until the entry
of Tiresias, but there are hints of their presence, both in choral
songs, and in the unusual dramatic technique. At the end of the
prologue, Antigone goes out to bury her brother. In the middle of
the first episode, the guard reports that the body has been lightly
covered with dust. There is no sign of who could have performed
the deed. The guard leaves under Creon's threats. When he returns
after the choral ode, he has captured Antigone. The guards had
uncovered the body and waited. A dust storm arose at noon, and
when it ended Antigone was beside the corpse, carrying out burial
rites. Polynices is thus buried twice.[14]

The first burial was complete, for the guard says that the doer
"performed the proper rites" (247). The description of it has a note
of the miraculous. Not only was there no trace of wagon, mattock,
or footprint, but no animal came close to the body. Each item can
be explained naturalistically.[15] The guard stresses the lack of tools,
since without his complicity a full-scale burial could hardly have
been accomplished. The burial took place at night, when vultures
do not hunt. Yet we are directed to see the event as wondrous. The
chorus first responds by suggesting that the gods are responsible
(278–79), and when Creon refutes this idea, they sing an ode about
human cunning, and the burial is doubtless the inspiring example.
The two responses render the burial problematic. As audience, we
have seen Antigone go to bury her brother, and we can hardly fail
to assume that the guard's report proves that she has succeeded. At
the same time, the report shows her attempt as amazingly successful.
Not only has she performed the burial without being captured, but
the thin layer of dust has protected the corpse.

Why then does she return? If Creon intended to denude the body
each time dust was placed on it, she would have no hope of keeping
it covered forever; and she has said that she will give up when the
task is beyond her ability (91). And Creon does not even order the
body uncovered; the guard does this on his own. She cannot expect
to keep the corpse physically covered, the ritual has been satisfac-
torily accomplished, and it is not at all clear how she knows what
has happened. The second burial is as uncanny as the first. Antigone
is hidden from the guards by the whirlwind of dust until she is
already beside the body; she has traveled to the body through a

storm during which the guards were forced to close their eyes. This
is an implicit miracle—just natural enough to explain Creon's failure
to see the gods at work. And if Antigone is aided by miraculous
help here, we may suspect she had it earlier. The first burial leaves
no trace behind; the doer disappears. For the second, the doer appears
as if from nowhere. In each case, divine help seems to enable Antigone to reach her goal.

The second burial is interrupted as she pours libations. In the
second half of the play, the corpse of Polynices is as effectively
exposed as it was effectively buried. The prophet announces that
carrion birds and dogs have polluted all the altars of Thebes (1016–
18). Once the control of the body is truly Creon's, his decision to
expose it to carrion animals is effectively carried out, and the con-
sequences fulfill themselves with astonishing speed.

So both Antigone and Creon succeed. Antigone can claim to have
buried Polynices (900–3), although Creon has caused the corpse to
be devoured by animals. Polynices is buried twice, then effectively
unburied until Creon finally gives him authoritative burial. Antigone's return to the body thus demands neither a psychological nor
a ritual reason. It is part of the divine management, by which the
gods participate in the human battle of wills. Like all divine actions,
it is beyond mortal explanation, and not entirely rational. The gods
help Antigone in her task. Yet the concealing dust disappears, and
once Antigone is captured, it is no longer Antigone's will they
fulfill, but Creon's. The double burial may be their message to
Creon, which he rejects because, just as he cannot imagine Haemon
as motivated both by love and by concern for himself, so he cannot
see the element of the miraculous in an act performed by a human
agent. But the gods do not speak directly. Nor do they protect
those who are loyal to them, as Antigone complains (921–24). They
only make human intentions effectual, and thus lead both principals
to destruction for reasons we cannot know.

The gods thus ensure that human actions have their widest con-
sequences. They justify Antigone's action, but that is not the only
reason the play invokes them, for the tragedy is not really about
the right or wrong of Polynices' burial. The drama shows how a
catastrophe overcomes the royal house of Thebes through a conjunction of causes; it depicts a world of moral complexity in which
Creon's reliance on reason is as mad as his son's erotic passion.
Antigone's rightness is a deeply ironic phenomenon: the right course

for the city is proclaimed by one who has no concern for the city. The tragedy points to the pathetic fragility of human institutions. Reason, celebrated in the "Ode on Man," is not infallible; Antigone's attachment to instinctual family ties is the correct guide. But Creon's fear of anarchy is not to be mocked, and Haemon shows that the conflicts of family and love can be as ruinous as those of family and authority. There are no easy solutions.

Chapter Five
A Hidden God:
Oedipus the King

Background and Plot

Several different kinds of background function in this play. On the one hand, the dramatic action consists of the gradual reconstruction of a series of past events: the play is the unraveling of its own prehistory. At the same time, the unrelenting dramatic irony depends on the spectator's knowledge of the story's outlines. Jocasta and Laius, the rulers of Thebes, learned from an oracle that their son would kill his father and marry his mother. When Jocasta bore a son, he was exposed. He was saved from death, however, and in ignorance killed Laius. When Thebes was afflicted by a monster, the Sphinx, who killed all who could not answer her riddle, he solved the riddle, and the pest killed herself. In reward Oedipus became king, and married his mother, Jocasta. Eventually he learned the truth. This legend was old and much treated when Sophocles composed his play (perhaps in the 420s),[1] and at some points he may be setting his version in contrast to specific predecessors.

The play opens with a tableau of suppliants before the palace represented by the stage building. The citizens seek the help of their king, Oedipus, against a plague which is ravaging Thebes. His reply expresses his compassion and responsible forethought: he has already sent Creon, Jocasta's brother, to consult Apollo's oracle at Delphi. Creon opportunely enters (78–79). The plague has arisen because the land is polluted by the murderer of the former king Laius. The slayer must be killed or exiled. Laius, according to the one slave who survived the incident, was killed by bandits while traveling on a sacred embassy. At the time it was assumed that the killers were agents of a political faction, but the Sphinx prevented investigation. Oedipus announces that he will search for the killer as a duty to Thebes, Laius, and himself.

The suppliants depart and the chorus of elders enters (151), wondering what the oracle will command. They pray to many gods for help against the plague, destroyer of fertility of land and women; identifying the plague with the war-god Ares, they call on the other gods to drive him away. Oedipus delivers a decree and a curse. If the killer confesses, he will be exiled and no more. If he and those who know him are silent, let them be constrained by Oedipus's curse: no one is to receive the killer, speak to him, or share religious rites with him. Oedipus cannot do less for the god and the man whose widow is his own wife than avenge Laius like a son. Let whoever disobeys suffer the plague and worse, but may the other Thebans be blessed. The chorus knows nothing—the god could tell. Oedipus responds that mortals cannot force the gods to speak, and the chorus suggests that he consult the prophet Tiresias. But on Creon's advice he has already sent for him during the entry-song, and Tiresias is now led in (300).

Though Oedipus addresses Tiresias with utmost respect, the prophet refuses to speak. At last Oedipus loses his temper and accuses Tiresias of being an accomplice; Tiresias replies that Oedipus is the killer. As Oedipus's accusations magnify, Tiresias's prophecies become ever clearer: Oedipus will be driven by his parents' curse, blind, equal to his own children. This day will give Oedipus birth and destroy him. His skill at riddles has ruined him. Oedipus replies that he does not care, if the city was saved, and enters the house as Tiresias predicts blindness and ruin at his back.[2] The chorus sings of the killer as a wanderer in the wild, a bull, pursued by the oracle. Still the singers are distressed by the prophecies. But all human prophecy is fallible, Oedipus had no enmity against Laius, and the king proved his virtue against the Sphinx. They will not blame him without proof.

Creon enters (513), having heard that Oedipus has accused him of conspiracy with Tiresias. A confrontation follows. Creon argues that he has no reason to conspire against Oedipus, since he now enjoys power without its disadvantages, but Oedipus is not convinced, and wants Creon executed. Jocasta enters (631–33) and rebukes them for squabbling amid civic grief. With the support of the chorus, she prevails on Oedipus to accept Creon's oath that he is innocent, though Oedipus still insists that relenting will ruin him. Both men are still angry when Creon exits.

Jocasta asks the cause of the quarrel, and tries to soothe Oedipus by pointing out that prophets are fallible: Laius, for instance, told by Apollo's servants that he would die at the hands of his son, was killed by robbers at the meeting of three roads, while the child, his ankles pierced, was exposed. Oedipus is disturbed and inquires about Laius's death—where it happened, when, what he looked like. Now he fears the prophet may see. He tells his story from the beginning. Son of Polybus and Merope of Corinth, he was told by a drunken man that he, Oedipus, was a bastard. Though his parents denied this, he went to Delphi to ask the oracle. Apollo told him he would kill his father and marry his mother. Resolving to avoid Corinth, he was pushed out of the road at a triple crossroads by an old man in a chariot who was attended by a herald and slaves. Oedipus killed the man and his attendants. Now he can only hope that the survivor will insist that there were many bandits. Jocasta reminds him that many heard him speak of several attackers, and insists that even if he changes his tale, the oracle was still false. The slave, now a herdsman, is sent for, and Oedipus goes indoors (861–62).

The chorus sings a prayer for purity in everything governed by eternal, divine law. *Hybris*—behavior without proper limits—creates the tyrant, and falls to ruin. May the gods destroy the wicked man who has no reverence and pursues unjust gains, touching the untouchable; otherwise, why join the dance in honor of the gods? And if the oracles are not proved true, how can the singers have faith? Apollo is no longer manifest in honor.

Jocasta comes from the house with offerings for Apollo, whose statue is by the door, praying for a "pure solution." A messenger enters (924): Polybus of Corinth has died. Oedipus, relieved, still fears that he might someday wed his mother. Jocasta tells him chance rules life, and oracles should be ignored, but the messenger tells him that Merope was not his mother; he himself was given Oedipus, a baby with pierced ankles, by a herdsman of Laius on Mt. Cithaeron. The chorus-leader thinks this man is also the survivor of Laius's murder. Jocasta now tries to convince Oedipus to give up his search, and when he refuses, exits calling him "miserable" (1071–72). He assumes she fears he is lowborn, but as the child of chance he will not be ashamed. The chorus sings of Cithaeron, where perhaps the king was born of a nymph, son of some god.

The summoned herdsman enters (1123). He will not speak, despite reminders from the Corinthian, until Oedipus threatens him with torture. Then he admits that the child he pitied too much to leave to wild animals was Laius's son. Oedipus rushes into the house, as the chorus sings of mortal fragility: Oedipus was the greatest of men, now he is nothing. A messenger describes how Oedipus burst into Jocasta's chamber. She had hanged herself. Oedipus took the brooches from her dress and put out his eyes. Oedipus himself comes out (1297) and laments with the chorus, defending his self-blinding—he had nothing good to see in this world or the next. Now he wishes only to be cast out.

Creon comes forth (1422) in order to bring Oedipus indoors. He will not drive Oedipus out without another consultation with the oracle. Oedipus's daughters are brought out, and he commends them to Creon's care. Once promised that he will be exiled when Apollo approves, Oedipus goes into the house.

Structure and Sources

A precise knowledge of epic and other variants of the myth is not possible, but fortunately probably also relatively unimportant for the play. Probably in the earliest versions of the story, Oedipus's identity was discovered immediately after his marriage, and his children were born of a second marriage; he remained king of Thebes after the discovery.[3] The end of Sophocles' play, with its hesitation about the exile of Oedipus, may allude to such variants.

Most important for Sophocles was surely the trilogy about the house of Laius produced by Aeschylus in 467, from which *Seven against Thebes* survives. While this trilogy placed Oedipus's meeting with his father at a triple crossroad, the junction was at Potniae, south of Thebes. The location of the encounter between Thebes and Delphi, one coming from the oracle, the other probably toward it, is probably a Sophoclean innovation. Most important is the treatment of the oracle. In Aeschylus Laius was warned by the god not to have a child, and disobeyed; Sophocles makes the oracle a neutral statement of fact. Moreover, Aeschylus's work was probably structured like the extant *Oresteia,* with repeated crime and retribution manifesting a familial curse. None of this appears in the *Oedipus.*[4]

In a brief allusion to the legend in the *Odyssey* (11. 274), we hear that the gods made the truth known. But for Sophocles, the plot is Oedipus's discovery of the truth; his play is a continual progress toward truth and a continual delaying action. The piece is a tour de force in which no possibility for irony is left undeveloped. Oedipus and others constantly allude to the truth unknowingly, as the audience, painfully aware of what Oedipus must learn, watches fragments of the truth appear as Oedipus misconstrues them. The revelation is brought close and then evaded: Tiresias speaks only when Oedipus is too angry to listen, and Jocasta sees before Oedipus does, but does not speak. Her silence recalls the literally silent exits of Deianeira and Eurydice, but unlike theirs is a function of plot as much as character.

Since Aristotle,[5] *Oedipus* has been admired for its success in uniting the unlikely events of Oedipus's life with the laws of probability and necessity. An impression of inevitable causality is joined with the terror of coincidence. There are two distinct levels in the play, the process of revelation on the surface, and the gradually revealed pattern of what is revealed. Coincidence links them through the roles of the two herdsmen—Laius's servant who saved Oedipus and was unconsciously requited by being spared at the killing of Laius, and the Corinthian who brought the baby to Polybus and comes to tell him that Polybus is dead. These doublings of function are implausible, perhaps, yet acceptable because they provide so elegant a structure. At the same time these are real, though minor characters. Jocasta tells us that the herdsman, seeing Oedipus as king, asked to be sent away from the city (758–64): his fear is a natural response and yet functional in delaying the recognition. The doubling of roles allows the shift of interest from the murder to Oedipus's parentage, and thus from parricide to incest, to happen easily, so that we never notice that the slave is not even questioned about Laius's murder: Oedipus's fate is such a unity that at the moment of understanding one truth subsumes the other.[6]

Within the drama itself each step is prepared naturally, so that the astonishing unlikelihoods are put into a credible framework. The modern reader is often surprised by the long speech in which Oedipus tells Jocasta his story (771–833), as if he had never mentioned the names of his parents, but stories in tragedy are often told from the beginning, repeating facts known to all, so that the formality of the conventional style conceals the unlikelihood of Oedipus's never having told his beloved wife basic facts—we do not know quite where his reticence began.[7] There is also one unmotivated entrance, that of the Corinthian. He, however, comes as an apparent answer to Jocasta's prayer for a "pure solution." Oedipus thinks perhaps Polybus died of grief for him and so fulfilled the oracle (969–70), as Jocasta suggests that many sleep with their mothers in dreams (981–82). The messenger with his trivial, unpolluting fulfillment seems to come as an answer from Apollo. He moreover appears to offer Oedipus an easy solution to the possibility that he killed Laius—he can return home to Corinth. But it is the discussion of this very issue—Oedipus's reason for avoiding Corinth—which begins the fatal revelation, and the turn comes through the messenger's natural desire to please his future king (1005–6). This apparently unmotivated entrance is thus doubly motivated, by the everyday reasons of the messenger and the god. In the end, Apollo cannot be separated from the pattern of coincidence.

Oedipus

Within the play, the basic dramatic problem is to delay Oedipus's discovery without straining credibility or allowing Oedipus, the great solver of riddles, to appear a fool. In part audience goodwill is required: we accept that he cannot find out too soon and take pleasure in the constant ironies. But more deeply, the process of discovery is curiously difficult, and the delays we see before us echo the events which brought Oedipus to his fate. Oedipus's life has been determined by oracular speech and silence, by human lies, by coincidence or divine will, and by his own nature. All these are at work in the action.

Oedipus is defined from the start as a solver of riddles, and the search for Laius's killer is explicitly compared to this achievement. Oedipus himself contrasts Tiresias's silence at that time with his activity; in solving riddles the prophet will find him great (441). The famous riddle asked what walks on four legs in the morning, two at midday, three at evening; the answer is "man." Oedipus himself may exemplify or violate the rule, with his pierced ankles as an infant: he will carry a staff in the prime of his life. The riddle is never quoted in the play, but puns on Oedipus's name, "Swollenfoot," are common.[8] The solution to the prior riddle saved the city; in solving the new riddle Oedipus will save the city again, yet reveal that it is he himself from whom the city must be saved. As solver he is savior, yet curse—for his original success led to his marriage

and establishment in Thebes; as object of the riddle he exemplifies
the human condition, and yet is outside it, exaggerating it.

All that was needed against the Sphinx was courage and intelligence. The first part of the play presents the energetic, concerned,
quick-witted Oedipus, who asks the advice of the chorus and turns
out to have done already what the elders suggest. He has faith in
intelligence, "One thing could uncover the understanding of many"
(120). His self-confidence is not impious. He will do all he can,
and the city will stand or fall "with god's help" (145–46). He
actively seeks divine counsel from Delphi and Tiresias. This Oedipus
of the opening scene embodies all that Athenians of the fifth century
liked to believe they were, and without standing for the city or its
leader, Pericles, he is an idealized Athenian, capable, rational, and
optimistic.[9]

In the encounter with Tiresias this changes. On the flimsiest of
evidence Oedipus creates a conspiracy against himself. Like the
similar scene in *Antigone,* the episode contrasts divine and human
knowledge, but Oedipus, though he behaves even worse than Creon,
is more sympathetic: the prophet seems to lack any pity for his
native city. When Tiresias finally speaks, Oedipus is too angry to
believe; here, as so often, he is confronted with obstinate reticence.
The failure of the encounter to lead to knowledge is the result of
both Tiresias's refusal to speak and Oedipus's fierce temper and
overquickness. Typically, it is Jocasta's attempt to prove that Tiresias's prophecies are unimportant which leads to her mention of
the crossroads and so proves their truth.

The vital clue of the crossroads ends the digression caused by the
imagined conspiracy, but submerges another clue. Jocasta tells her
story in a confused order, describing first Laius's death, then the
exposure of the baby (715–19). Stunned by the first detail, Oedipus
does not hear the second or connect it with his injury of foot. He
concentrates on one thing at a time. Just as Tiresias's resistance led
him to imagine a conspiracy between Creon and Tiresias, and he
could then not really hear what Tiresias said, so once the detail he
recalls strikes him, all his attention is there. And the next twist
again diverts him. The discrepancy in the number of killers allows
Laius's murder to be temporarily put aside. "One could not be equal
to many" (845). Of course, he is the exception, at once husband
and son, father and brother. But the doubt allows his attention to
turn entirely to the issue of parentage.

The obstacles in his path are many: the information given by the god is scanty, and he cannot be forced to tell more (280–81); Tiresias will not speak until too late; the herdsman lied about the number; Jocasta tells her story in the wrong order; Oedipus himself is too hot-tempered and too ready to look only at the immediate question. At the same time, his will to know pushes the action forward. The qualities of the drama are thus those of Oedipus's fate as a whole. When Oedipus asked Polybus and Merope whether they were his natural parents, they lied to him. When he asked the oracle for the truth about his parentage, the god denied him the answer, but told him a different truth. Laius provoked him at the crossroads as Tiresias provokes him on stage, and his violent temper each time reveals itself. His reaction to Apollo's evasive reply is to assume, apparently, that his doubts about his parentage were unfounded, just as Tiresias's behavior makes him leap to a wrong conclusion. The Oedipus of the past won his natural place as king of Thebes by his skill at riddles; the same process now unravels the earlier events.

Guilt

The issue of responsibility cannot be avoided, unless we join the small group of those who have denied that the play is more than a thrilling detective story, an exploitation of the terror of coincidence.[10] There can be no doubt that the ironies the plot allows are exploited for their own sake when Oedipus speaks of Laius's killer as his own enemy, or when he stresses that he is foreign to the city, a stranger to the affair of the murder (219–22). He considers his marriage to Laius's widow a special tie. And the great self-directed curse is spectacular theater. But we can hardly believe that the way the action is structured as a test of the oracles is merely a way of generating further ironies.

On the other hand, the moral of the tragedy can hardly be that all oracles are true (Sophocles' friend Herodotus could have disproved any such naive assertion) or that Oedipus and Jocasta are justly punished for doubting them.[11] For when the two reject the oracles, they have already been fulfilled, and to believe the oracle would be simply to accept the punishment as inevitable without the crime. Moreover, Oedipus's belief in oracular revelation is the basis of the action. Ironically, it is the characters' faith in oracles which leads to their misfortunes as they try to avoid what has been predicted for them. This attempt is, of course, no sin. The god has not said what he wants, but only what will happen, and the fulfillment may take a strange form. Mortals do what they can to avert disaster, and hope that the fulfillment may be merely symbolic. But the characters' faith in oracles ultimately supports Jocasta's advice, "to live at random, as best one can" (979)—not because oracles are false, as she thinks, but because they are self-fulfilling.

In her first reference to oracles, Jocasta distinguishes between Apollo and his mortal servants (712). Her argument is that mortals have no share in prophetic art, a possibility already raised by the conventional chorus. Later she lets this distinction slip (853), just as the distinction between an oracle's being false and its being trivially fulfilled is muddled. The chorus believes that the worship of the gods depends on belief in oracles (897–910), but she partially refutes their song by appearing at its close with offerings for Apollo. The chorus apparently distinguishes a prophet like Tiresias and the Delphic oracle: a seer can be wrong, but not the great prophetic shrines. Jocasta is not concerned with this difference. She rather asserts that a god "will himself easily show forth" what he enjoins (724–25). Like the Creon of *Antigone,* she is overrational in divine matters. She and Oedipus reject the oracles for pious reasons: they assume that a god who could speak clearly would not speak ambiguously. Jocasta would have faith in a completely unmediated divine word, but epiphanies are very rare. She believes in chance, Oedipus in reason; but her error is not unlike his, when he assumed that Polybus and Merope were his parents because the oracle did not directly answer his question about them. Both think that gods and mortals reason compatibly, so that they could understand the gods. They are naive. Yet oracles are no use unless the recipient thinks he can interpret them. A mortal must neither reject an oracle nor imagine he understands it.

This innocence of Oedipus about the dark ways of the gods is a real factor in his calamity: his mistake is deeper than the issue of belief or skepticism. There is a second point at which his responsibility becomes an issue. He is manifestly unjust to Tiresias and Creon. Again his actual disaster has already taken place, and so can hardly be divine vengeance for these acts, but his behavior within the drama recalls his earlier actions. Oedipus was not the aggressor in the encounter with Laius; his rage is provoked, as within the play Tiresias provokes him. Indeed, the scene at the crossroads is described as a gradual escalation (803–14): first Laius and his herald push Oedipus; Oedipus strikes the herald and tries to pass; Laius strikes Oedipus with his goad; Oedipus kills the entire party. Yet Oedipus himself describes Laius's payment for his insult as "unequal" and the person of a herald was sacred (like that of Tiresias). Creon describes Oedipus's rage as a product of his inborn nature, *physis* (674–75): "Such natures are most painful for themselves to bear." In each of his angry encounters in the play, Oedipus quarrels with one with whom he is to exchange roles—he will be blind like Tiresias, Creon will be king instead of Oedipus. With Laius this is even stronger. Laius is the source of Oedipus's *physis*, Oedipus physically resembles his father (743), he will replace him as ruler of Thebes, and their characters are alike. Pride and anger meet in their meeting. The nature of Oedipus is a necessary component of his fate.

Nonetheless, while Oedipus's character is one cause of his misfortunes, it hardly justifies them. Although Oedipus is destroyed in part because he misunderstands the gods, leaps too rapidly to conclusions, and is violent and hot-tempered, nowhere is it really suggested that these errors were foreseen and punished by the gods. The one passage which might lead to such an interpretation is the choral song which follows the dispute with Creon and Jocasta's rejection of oracles (863–910). Here the elders express their fears of *hybris* and predict its fall, and pray for the validation of the oracles. Their prayers condemn Oedipus, who is the evildoer they describe, who has not kept himself from unholy deeds, and who will be ruined by the confirmation of the oracles. Their language is such that it continually describes Oedipus (there is even a pun on his name), and yet seems askew, since the words more naturally refer to a conscious sinner, one who despises justice and the gods. The deeds of Oedipus place him in the category the chorus curses: if anyone acts thus, let an evil fate take him! Yet an evil fate has already taken him in unwittingly doing the deeds for which he is cursed. The song's reaffirmation of the divine law shows that Oedipus must fall. But it only deepens the moral ambiguity of the drama. The impulse for the song is Oedipus's tyrannical behavior toward Creon and the rejection of oracles. Its language points to the parricide and incest, of which the singers are ignorant (even as simple murder the killing of Laius is still uncertain). Yet the choral assumption that sin is deliberate and conscious undercuts the applicability of the moral scheme to Oedipus. There is a terrible disparity between the level at which he is actually responsible, the deeds he has committed, and their moral connotations. The elders ask why they should dance, if wickedness is honored, but the question is harder than they know. If Oedipus's errors require the divine vengeance of which the chorus sings, why must they dance?

Fate

Oedipus's character is necessary for the disaster, and he acts freely both within the drama and in the events he recounts. He is no puppet. Still we cannot say that Apollo has no essential part in what happens to Oedipus. The oracles are a truth outside time, and Apollo's knowledge of what will happen does not imply that he wills the events. Apollo, however, does not merely know the future, but also imparts his knowledge, and not mechanically, but according to his will. Early in the play, Oedipus reminds the chorus that no man can force a god (280–81). When he realizes that he may have killed Laius, he joins this fear with the fact that he cannot return to Corinth for fear of the oracle, attributing this fear to a "cruel divinity" (828–29). The following prayer, in which he twice prays not to "see" such disaster (830–34) will be in a sense answered by the self-blinding; gods who answer prayer thus seem cruel indeed.

The oracle to Laius is described by Jocasta as having "come" to him (711). No solicitation is mentioned. When Oedipus asked the oracle the identity of his parents, he was "dishonored" (789) in what he came for. In a sense, of course, Apollo has replied. Yet in each case the oracle is not a neutral response to a question; the divine message intrudes or evades. This active role in the past is repeated in the present. Though Apollo is never explicitly called the sender of the plague, he is a god of plague. The plague is not simply a result of the ritually polluting presence of Oedipus, coming when he has ruled for so long; it is a divine intervention, arbitrary as such can be—the god acts when he will. Tiresias explicitly says (376–77): "It is not your fate to fall at my hands, since Apollo is sufficient, who is concerned to accomplish this." Near the end Oedipus refers his self-blinding to Apollo, though he struck the blow himself (1329–30). The god is not neutral; Oedipus is right to call himself "hateful to divinity" (816).

We cannot call Apollo's treatment of Oedipus personal malevolence. While he, like other gods, is normally seen as acting under recognizably human motives, supporting his worshippers, and taking drastic revenge on any who slight him, there is no hint whatever in the play that the god was angry at Oedipus. Apollo has only two functions: he gives the oracles, and he forces the truth to light. The oracles stand both within and outside ordinary causality. They cause the fate they predict, and in any case they are infallibly true. Once the oracle is given, the future is inescapable. But we cannot know whether the oracles merely report events already fixed in the allotment of things *(Moira)* or whether Apollo, by speaking the inevitable, creates it. [12]

Jocasta contrasts the oracles with *Tyche* ("Chance"), the randomness in events. To attribute an event to chance does not necessarily mean that it has no cause, but only that the cause is beyond the speaker's knowledge or control. Jocasta is arguing that human foresight is so limited that neither oracles nor rational planning is effective when she says "best live at random" (979). When Oedipus thinks he will be shown to be of low birth, he calls himself "son of *Tyche*" (1080). He is the exposed infant who became a prince, then the exile who won a kingdom. The emphasis is a reminder of the role of pure coincidence in the story: the drunken taunt or the meeting with Laius. Within the play the death of Polybus at this time seems to be mere *Tyche,* and Jocasta so calls it (949). Yet the arrival of the messenger who reports this death seems to answer her prayer. Much in life appears as chance, since mortals cannot decipher each causal chain as it comes to touch themselves. Whether the apparently chance elements in Oedipus's story are truly chance, or the disguised work of *Moira,* is never certain.

The play is not a tragedy of fate. Not only does the protagonist act freely, but his own character is essential to events. The oracles set in motion a group of free mortals whose encounters are governed partly by their own choices, partly by apparent chance. As so often, causes seem to be both divine and human. Apollo is evasive, and mortals lie. Apollo and Oedipus are, as Oedipus claims, allies (245).

Intelligence

At the center of the drama is Oedipus with his absolute determination to know the truth. He dominates from beginning to end.

The paradox which divides interpreters and renders the play so perpetually fascinating is how the mind of Oedipus both succeeds and fails. The work proves how frail mortals are; all his energy and skill have only brought him ruin, and the chorus takes him as an example of why nothing in the world can be called blessed (1186–96). The prophet is right in saying that skill at riddles ruined him (442). Yet this response to the claim of Oedipus to be great in this above all does not cancel what Oedipus has said, and Oedipus also claims not to care if his skill ruined himself, since he saved Thebes. Both the errors of the search and the final discovery display the limits of human ability, but Oedipus does at least find the truth he seeks.

In the scene with the herdsman, Oedipus evidently knows before the final word is spoken. The very struggle of the slave to avoid telling what he knows reveals how dreadful it is. Oedipus here is angry for the last time in the play, and his anger is again directed at one who withholds the truth from him. But this time, as he is closer to ruin he is also far closer to truth, and his anger attains its goal. When Oedipus threatens to torture the old man, the point is not his cruelty but his rage to learn what he realizes is a terrible truth. When at last the slave cries out that he is on the verge of horror and about to declare it, Oedipus replies almost gently (1170): "And I of hearing. But still I must hear." Oedipus insists on the truth, and in winning the truth in some sense makes it his own.

The self-blinding fulfills the prediction of Tiresias, and Oedipus attributes it to Apollo (1329–30). But not only is the hand Oedipus's own, he later defends the deed to the chorus in fully rational, human terms. He is still the winner of arguments; in the last lines of dialogue, Creon reproaches him with seeking to rule as he always has (1522–23). Abject though he is at some moments near the end of the drama, Oedipus does not draw from his life the moral drawn by the chorus. Rather he affirms his individuality. He encourages the chorus to cast him out, kill him, or hurl him into the sea without fearing to touch him (his pollution would resemble a contagious disease in the eyes of most): none can bear the evils of Oedipus but himself (1414–15). Even his pollution is peculiarly his own. And he is convinced that he will not perish on Cithaeron, where he wishes to be sent to die as he was long ago saved there, either of disease or any other natural cause. For he would not have been saved unless for some uncanny and terrible fate (1455–58). In blindness he attains something like prophecy. The discovery, horrible as it is, is satisfying for both protagonist and audience. Accepting his fate, Oedipus is in accordance with the gods, even as he insists that they hate him (1519), and he is still himself. Even as it portrays mortal limitation and blindness, the fate of Oedipus also culminates in a discovery the character seeks and accepts. The pattern of disaster is what intelligence wins, and it is a real, though awful prize.

The End of the Play

Throughout the play it is Oedipus who initiates action. The search and discovery are his, and even when most wrong he controls the action. The prologue, in which he emerges alone to hear the suppliants' plea, and reenters the palace when they depart, establishes his stature. He next enters to deliver his edict. His exit, with Tiresias addressing him as he goes, is a moral defeat, but a defeat of his choice: he refuses to hear more. In the following scene, Creon's entrance leads to his, as he emerges in surprise that Creon dares show himself. The chorus urges Jocasta to "bring this man indoors" after the dispute (678), but they do not go in until 862. Oedipus cannot be driven into the house, away from the truth; when he enters the acting space again, he does not exit until he knows. It is Jocasta who rushes inside (1071–72); Oedipus remains through the song celebrating his birth and himself signals the herdsman's approach (1110–13). Oedipus always comes and goes through the palace door, while the messengers of the outside world—Creon, Tiresias, the Corinthian, the herdsman—enter along the side-aisles, the *parodoi*. But Tiresias declares that Oedipus will become a blind beggar, and Oedipus has decreed his own exile. The audience is led to expect that at the end of the play Oedipus will go into exile, exiting down a *parodos*. This does not happen.

Instead Creon insists that Oedipus go indoors and wait for a further consultation of the oracle. Oedipus wishes to display himself to all (1287–91) and to fulfill his curse, while Creon claims that if he does not revere humanity, the sun should be spared the sight of Oedipus (1424–31). Only the family should see or hear such intimate pains. Creon is not cruel; he sends for Oedipus's daughters, and does not mock him. And his decision to wait for a further message from Apollo is reasonable, for the drama has shown how dangerous quick conclusions about oracles can be. Yet this end, with Oedipus brought back into the house, is somehow wrong. Not just Oedipus, but the whole drama opposes it, and we can hardly fail to think that the house and family have seen more than they should already.

The ending may have been contrived as a way of reconciling the variant traditions about what happened to Oedipus by leaving the issue in doubt. Still, the end is very much an anticlimax; like *Ajax, Oedipus the King* ends in a diminished world. There are hints of trouble to come. Oedipus refers to his grown sons, who can care for themselves, while placing his young daughters under Creon's protection and lamenting their sad future. The sufferings still in store are thus imprecisely suggested, though there is no allusion to *Antigone* or any other specific work. Creon promises Oedipus that he will be exiled when the god permits; the promised conclusion is only delayed. Still, the spectator is deprived of the feeling of liberation which would come with the departure of Oedipus. There is something disturbing in the loss of control over the action by the protagonist at the point at which he at last has full understanding and desires with full knowledge to follow the decree of the gods. While we may have forgotten the plague by now, its cure was to be the death or exile of the killer, and we cannot but feel Oedipus's urgency. Until he goes, the story is not over. As in the other plays of Sophocles, the end is a reminder that this drama has shown only part of a longer story. The refusal of closure is perturbing, and is meant to be: led to expect a cruel but satisfying exit into exile, we are left only with a reentry into a house which has already seen too much.

Chapter Six
Word and Deed: *Electra*

Myth and Plot

The story of the House of Atreus has been among the most popular myths both in antiquity and in modern times, and especially the stories of Agamemnon and his children. Agamemnon sacrificed his daughter Iphigeneia to the goddess Artemis when she becalmed the Greek army at Aulis, so that it could not sail for Troy. In his long absence, his wife Clytemnestra took a lover, Aegisthus, and the pair killed Agamemnon on his return. Orestes, Agamemnon's son, grew up in exile and at last came home and killed Aegisthus and his mother with the help of his sister, Electra. In the version established by Aeschylus's *Oresteia,* he was pursued by the avenging goddesses, the Furies, until he was acquitted by an Athenian court (the god Apollo, whose oracle ordered the killings, was his advocate).[1]

Sophocles' play opens as Orestes' old paedagogue identifies for the newly returned Orestes the sights of his native city. It is dawn. The old man, Orestes, and Orestes' friend Pylades (a silent character) must make their plans. Orestes sets forth his scheme: when he asked Apollo at Delphi how he should take revenge, he was told to take his just vengeance by guile. Therefore the old man, who will not be recognized after so long, is to tell the usurpers that Orestes has died in the Pythian Games; the friends will visit Agamemnon's tomb, and then come to the palace disguised as the bearers of Orestes' ashes. A lamenting voice is heard from within, and Orestes wonders if this is not Electra, but the paedagogue urges him not to wait. They depart, and Electra emerges from the house (86).

She sings a lament for her father and curses his killers. The chorus of local women enters (121) and in lyric dialogue try to console Electra. Though the women sympathize with her in hating the criminals, they remind her that grief is futile, fighting with the stronger foolish, and that Zeus will help Orestes' return. The same themes are continued in spoken form, as Electra admits that she is ashamed if she laments too much, but her life of dependence on her enemies is unbearable. At present she can speak freely only because Aegisthus is away. Chrysothemis, her sister, now comes from the house with offerings (325–27). She warns Electra that Aegisthus plans to imprison her beyond the borders of the land; but Electra answers that she would prefer such a fate to her present life, and what is sensible yielding to force in her sister's eyes is flattery in hers. Now Chrysothemis explains the offerings: during the night Clytemnestra dreamed that Agamemnon returned to life. He took his scepter and planted it by the hearth, and it grew a branch which overshadowed the land. Frightened by the dream, Clytemnestra is sending her obedient daughter with offerings to appease Agamemnon. Electra persuades her sister to throw the offerings aside and instead give Agamemnon locks of the sisters' hair, with a prayer that he aid their vengeance.

Chrysothemis goes to the tomb (471), and the chorus sings of how the Fury will come to the partners in adultery and murder. The song ends with a recollection of the chariot-race of Pelops. Oenomaus promised his daughter Hippodameia to whoever defeated him in a race. His charioteer, Myrtilus, removed the linch-pin from his chariot, so that Pelops was victorious; but Pelops threw Myrtilus into the sea, and his dying curse has allowed no end to the trouble of Pelops's descendants. Clytemnestra comes out of the palace (516) and upbraids her daughter for standing outside (respectable Greek women stayed indoors). Clytemnestra defends her killing of Agamemnon: he had murdered her daughter. Electra insists that her confession that she killed her husband is shameful, even if the killing was just, and that if revenge is right, Clytemnestra must be the next victim. But Iphigeneia's sacrifice was imposed on Agamemnon. In any case, Clytemnestra's arguments are pretense, as her marriage to Aegisthus proves. Perhaps Electra could justly be called foul-tongued or shameless; but at least she does not shame her mother's heritage in being so. The debate ends in threats. Electra is silent as her mother prays to Apollo for a happy life amid wealth and those children who honor her.

The paedagogue enters (660) to announce Orestes' death in a long description of the fictitious chariot-race in which he was killed. Clytemnestra's response is mixed, but she welcomes the messenger who has freed her from fear and brings him into the palace as Electra evokes Orestes' avenging spirit. Electra laments: she will be a slave to the murderers forever. Chrysothemis returns from the tomb (871),

filled with joy: a lock of hair and other offerings were at the tomb—
Orestes must have returned. Electra tells her that Orestes is dead.
Now she asks her sister's help. She wants to kill Aegisthus herself.
As long as he lives, Agamemnon's daughters will not be allowed
to marry, but if they act, they will not only show filial piety, but
will win husbands by their nobility. Chrysothemis is shocked, and
considers Electra's daring folly. She exits, and the chorus sings
Electra's praise.

Orestes and Pylades enter with the urn (1098–99). Electra begs
to be allowed to hold the urn, and Orestes, seeing that this woman
loves Orestes, gives it to her. She speaks a long lament for the
brother she cared for, wishing to join him and have rest. Orestes
can no longer restrain himself, as he recognizes her; he takes away
the urn over her protests, then reveals himself and shows her Agamemnon's signet. Electra sings for joy as he tries to quiet her; at
last the old man comes outside (1326) and warns the pair to be still
and act. They enter, and the chorus sings of the Furies who have
entered the house to take revenge. Electra comes out to watch for
Aegisthus's return, and cries are heard from within as Clytemnestra
begs uselessly for pity. Orestes and Pylades come out. All is well,
according to Orestes, if Apollo prophesied well (1424–25). Now
Aegisthus is seen coming, and the men again go within.

Electra tells Aegisthus that the body of Orestes has been brought,
and he calls for the gates to be opened and the corpse revealed to
any citizens who had had hopes of Orestes. A shrouded body is
revealed, and he lifts the veil, saying he wishes to lament one who
was his relative, although he sees the work of divine justice here.
He uncovers the body of Clytemnestra (1475). He seeks to speak,
but Electra demands that he be killed immediately and given such
a burial as he deserves. Orestes forces him into the house. Aegisthus
asks whether the house must see all the woes, present and future,
of the children of Pelops; Orestes replies that it will see his, at least.
If all evildoers were killed, wickedness would be rare. They enter,
and the chorus salutes the children who have won freedom at last.

Text and Subtext

If *Antigone* is in many ways the easiest work of Sophocles to
approach, *Electra,* so obviously similar in its central figure, is surely
the most difficult. There are no ready, abstract "themes"; instead

there is a brilliant re-treatment of the dramatic subject.[2] All the plays of Sophocles are filled with echoes and allusions, but *Electra* seems more than any other composed always with its great predecessor, Aeschylus's *Libation Bearers,* behind each action. The *Oresteia,* of which *Libation Bearers* is the second play, was an immediate classic after its production in 458. It may have been revived about 420, for both Euripides and Sophocles wrote revisions of the play. Sophocles' play is close in style to his *Philoctetes* of 409, while that of Euripides would be dated on metrical grounds to ca. 417, but is dated by many scholars to 413 because of an allusion to "Sicilian seas," taken by some as a reference to the Sicilian expedition.[3] Both plays alter the dramatic focus of the Aeschylean original by concentrating on Electra. In *Libation Bearers* she is a secondary figure. Sent to the tomb of Agamemnon with offerings because her mother has dreamed of giving birth to a serpent, she prays instead for the return of Orestes. She sees the signs left by Orestes' visit to the tomb, and soon Orestes himself comes forth. After the recognition, the two sing a lament to rouse the shade of Agamemnon to their aid. But once the plan of the murder is formed, Electra has no further part. The drama is the drama of Orestes. It is he who is driven both by his need to recover his ancestral place and by Apollo's oracle, he who announces his own death to his mother, and he who kills first Aegisthus, then Clytemnestra. And it is he who leaves at the end, driven by the Furies.

Both later tragedians shift their attention to Electra, and thus away from the physical action of the matricide to its antecedents. From the beginning Orestes' slaying of the usurpers was a rescue of his sister. For Sophocles and Euripides, however, the center is the woman to be rescued. For Euripides there is no escape. His Electra has been married to a poor farmer, who has, however, respected her virginity. The play is set in the country, and the protagonist is isolated from every reality: neither married nor unmarried, she refuses to take part in religious festivals and nurses romantic images of Orestes. She and Orestes are together for much of the first part without his revealing himself to her, and the recognition is brought about by an old slave of Agamemnon's. She has to push Orestes to the matricide, and entices her mother with a lie, not that of Orestes' death used by Aeschylus and Sophocles, but with the tale that she has had a baby. The will behind the murders is hers, and she shares in the terrible remorse which follows the matricide.

In Euripides' play the recognition is delayed simply by Orestes' failure to reveal himself. Electra is told of the signs of a visitor at Agamemnon's tomb—signs which in Aeschylus immediately prepared the recognition—but she argues that they do not prove anything. Sophocles' Electra also refuses to believe the signs, but only because she has already been told that Orestes is dead. The recognition is delayed because the siblings have no contact. Euripides' Orestes overhears his sister's opening monody, while Sophocles' character is forbidden to listen by the old man, so that Orestes and Electra do not meet until the scene in which each recognizes the other. Orestes does not know his sister until hearing her lament; her physical condition is far worse than he had imagined. "So I never knew my own sorrows," he says (1185). The first part of the drama is a play of incomplete mediations and intersecting strands.

In *Libation Bearers,* Clytemnestra's dream causes her to send Electra to the tomb, where she meets Orestes. There it is decided that Orestes and Pylades will go to the palace as Phocian strangers and ask for Aegisthus. After this preparation, there is a theatrical surprise when Clytemnestra greets the guests, and a further shock when Orestes announces his own death. This lie is dropped by Euripides; Sophocles expands it, devoting much of his drama to its effects on Electra. At the same time the dream—also dropped by Euripides—is made the vehicle not of the meeting, but of a garbled message, as Electra is put into the same situation in which Oedipus was placed, given truths only when he cannot believe.

Electra has a note of simple delight in virtuosity as a brilliant variant on a very familiar myth. But it is natural to look for particular significance in those elements which stand in special contrast with their counterparts in Aeschylus: the change in the content and dramatic function of the dream; the emphasis on deception; the change in the order of the killings (both Euripides and Aeschylus have Aegisthus killed first); the failure of the Furies to manifest themselves. At each point we find the traditional material rearranged and re-created.

The Dream

Clytemnestra's dream initiates an entire strand of action, one which occupies a large part of three scenes and requires a character of its own, Chrysothemis (a figure elsewhere no more than a name). None of this action is directly related to the murder plot. Orestes is not even told about it. Nonetheless, it is carefully structured within the play. In the first part, the dream motivates the successive entrances of Chrysothemis and Clytemnestra. Their encounters with Electra are parallel. Both begin by commenting on the fact that Electra is outdoors, in public (328–29, 516–18). Both women appear from the palace bearing offerings. Both scenes are essentially debates. Electra, indeed, reproaches her sister with speaking rebukes taught by her mother, and not her own (343–44). The meetings are thus explicitly related; the second is a more direct version of the other. And both end with prayer.

Chrysothemis is, of course, a tool of the same kind as Ismene. Like Ismene, she admits that her sister is essentially right, but considers it foolish to oppose superior force. The contrast is visually much stronger in *Electra,* however, for Chrysothemis is evidently rewarded for her subservience by better maintenance (359–62); she looks like a princess, while Electra can be taken for a servant. The similarity with *Antigone* is underlined by the proposal to bury Electra alive (379–82) in order to end her laments; she too is devoted to the dead. Chrysothemis, however, is persuaded by Electra to act as her intermediary; her request that Chrysothemis pray against her mother rather than for her is pious, according to the chorus, and just in her own opinion (464, 466–67).

Aeschylus's Clytemnestra dreamed of giving birth to a serpent, which bit her as she suckled it. The image is violent and darkly sexual, and it emphasizes the unnatural quality of a child who turns against his mother. The dream of Sophocles' character, on the other hand, is fully positive in its implications. It begins with a resurrection of Agamemnon (417–19). He plants his scepter at the hearth. The scepter is an obvious symbol of his royal power, and Chrysothemis mentions that Aegisthus now carries it; we are reminded that Aegisthus is a political usurper as well as a murderer. From the scepter springs a fruitful branch which shades the land. The dream recalls those of Xerxes and Astyages in Herodotus (7.19, 1.108), where spreading foliage represents imperial power. The scepter is apparently inspired by the oath of Achilles,[4] where the oath is apparently to be as sure as it is sure that the scepter will not send forth new shoots. The flowering is a miracle. Moreover, Aeschylus's Clytemnestra uses the image of shady foliage from a surviving root for Agamemnon's return from Troy in a hypocritical speech of welcome.[5] Clearly the dream means that Orestes will rule in his father's house and kingdom. Clytemnestra reacts to the dream with the same fear which her model felt at the more explicitly threatening dream of tradition.

Electra encourages Chrysothemis to pray that Agamemnon come himself as a helper and that Orestes live and triumph over his enemies (454–56). Clytemnestra prays to the statue of Apollo by the palace door that she may live in her wealth with her present friends (648–54). As her prayer ends, the old man enters with the false report of Orestes' death. The technique is like that of *Oedipus the King,* a messenger who seems an answer to prayer. This messenger, of course, seems to those within the action to fulfill Clytemnestra's prayers, while the spectator realizes that his appearance is a stage in the fulfillment of Electra's. Indeed, the fulfillment of her prayer is underway before it is made.

Literally, the prayer is never made, for Chrysothemis is too surprised by the signs of Orestes' visit to the tomb to perform the ritual. The offerings of the sisters, who could pray for their brother's return, are in effect subsumed in those of the brother himself. Chrysothemis' return is a dramatic surprise, for the intervening entrance of the paedagogue has made us forget her and brought the action to an apparently higher level: the intrigue has begun, yet we are brought back to signs and prayers. But the moral action of Electra is perhaps even more important thatn the physical action of Orestes. The second Electra-Chrysothemis scene is an exploitation of the ironic pathos of the situation for its own sake, but there are elements of greater import also. Electra's mistaken belief that her brother is dead leads her to propose that she and her sister kill Aegisthus. The scene elegantly recalls the first debate of the sisters, in which Electra persuaded Chrysothemis to help her, though not to join her in her rebellious attitude. This time, however, the risks are too great. Electra's arguments point back to the dream. She reminds Chrysothemis that they will be unable to marry as long as Aegisthus lives (959–72), and that they are deprived of their ancestral wealth. The conclusion of the dramatic results of the dream thus echoes the dream's message: the victory of the children will at last restore fertility to the house.

But Electra's resolve to kill Aegisthus herself is also a crucial moment in her essential function, that of linking the dead and the living. She urges Chrysothemis to labor with her father and brother (986–87). For her, the living are the agents of the dead and hardly to be separated from them; she prays for the help of Agamemnon and of Orestes in the same breath in the first scene with Chrysothemis. In the second she imagines that Orestes' own offerings to his father are offerings in memory of Orestes (932–33). This mistake reveals a basic truth. The dream presents an Orestes who is his father's son only. Father and son are almost the same; after the recognition, Electra says that she would not be astonished to see Agamemnon himself (1316–17). Throughout the first part of the play, Electra's chief activity has been ceaseless lamentation. It is this continual lament to which the chorus objects in the entry-song; the women remind Electra that she cannot bring her father back to life (138–39). Moreover, it is to her laments that those in power object (379). Ordinarily, the lament bridges the gap between living and dead in order to enable the dead to depart. Electra's laments, however, have the opposite function. They raise the dead.[6] The theme is taken from *Libation Bearers,* but altered in two significant ways. Electra's purpose, unlike that of her counterpart, is not literally to raise the spirit of the dead. Her ceaseless laments are the expression of her deepest self, not magical conjurations. Yet they seem, ultimately, to reach the other world, answered in Orestes. Second, Electra laments alone, though the chorus occasionally echoes her notes. The great lament which raises the dead in Aeschylus is sung by Electra, Orestes, and chorus together as a communal act. Electra is a typically Sophoclean protagonist in her isolation.

The Death of Orestes

Electra brings Orestes back as a new Agamemnon. It is therefore not insignificant that the mainspring of the other strand of action is Orestes' false death. In Aeschylus this lie is introduced as a surprise, and serves to motivate Clytemnestra's sending for Aegisthus and to reveal the ambivalence of Clytemnestra's feelings toward her son. Euripides does not employ the theme. But Sophocles' drama expands it, and the subject receives a separate introduction, as Orestes defends the strategy (59–64):

In what way does it pain me, when dying in word I am saved and win glory? I believe no word is bad, if profit comes with it. For I have seen in the past, often, even wise men die falsely, in word; then, when they come back home, they have greater honor.

This speech is not a defense of the use of deceit as such; that is sanctioned by the express bidding of Apollo. Rather it is directed at the ill-omened nature of a statement that one is dead; superstition suggests that such words tend to make themselves true. And Orestes' language does not actually deny the thought, though he is not afraid: his death will take place, though only "in word." The examples of the wise men doubtless include Odysseus, but also probably figures whose disappearances were self-proclaimed journeys to the under-world, Pythagoras or the Thracian, Zalmoxis.[7] For the skeptic, these men's tales were mere lies, but there is a real ambiguity. A mere lie merges into a real journey which is, nonetheless, not death.

Orestes instructs the paedagogue to say that he has died by accident in the Pythian Games at Delphi by falling from his chariot. When the message is delivered, the speech is exceptionally long, a virtuoso specimen of narrative. We are told that on the first day of the games Orestes was the victor in every event. On the second was the chariot race. All the entrants and their teams are carefully described. Orestes stayed behind for the first part of the race, "putting his trust in the end" (735). He successfully avoided a crash which destroyed all his competitors except an Athenian. The two raced neck and neck until, apparently, the final round, when Orestes struck the turning-post and was thrown to his death, dragged by the horses until no one of his friends would be able to recognize his mangled body. The elaboration of the speech is out of proportion to its apparent function, and it is unclear how the speech works.

Some critics have suggested that in listening to this vivid account we actually forget that it is not true, so that we can sympathize fully with Electra's grief, while others have insisted that we can hardly forget that the whole story is false, for we have been told what the lie will be.[8] The speech, in fact, poses a question about our response to fiction: we know, after all, that nothing in the drama is literally true, yet respond to it emotionally nonetheless. The speech seems to exploit basic human responses to fiction. Within a story, a lie whose status we know is, in effect, another story, and *Electra* is already haunted by the other possible versions of the story it tells. From the privileged position of the spectator, we enjoy the irony of the lie; we know better than the characters which version of the tale they present; yet the lie may possess some of the same kinds of truth as the drama itself.

Orestes is the agent of his dead father, and the two are closely identified by the dream and by Electra. There is thus an inner rightness in his recovery of his native land through an imitation death. He is "the crafty-footed ally of those below" (1391–92), led into the house by Hermes, who is both the patron of guile and the guide of the dead. Thus confusions between living and dead are prominent in the latter part of the drama. Electra laments over the urn as her brother stands alive beside her, while Aegisthus approaches the body he believes is that of Orestes, only to uncover Clytemnestra. Electra has early in the play complained (244–50):

If the dead will lie as earth and nothing, miserable, and *they* do not pay a penalty of blood in exchange, reverence and piety would vanish from all humanity.

Through his death in word, Orestes becomes a fitting agent to prove that the dead man is not mere earth.

But the report of the false death points also other ways. Sophocles alone among the tragedians places the family curse in the chariot race of Pelops, and the death of Orestes in such a race is surely intended to recall that earlier event. The meaning of the allusion is ambiguous, however. It could mean that the fictitious death of the last hope of the family is the final blow of the curse; the story brings the troubles of the house to an end. Yet it could be read in an opposite sense, as a reminder that the curse is active still. Again, the entire speech is a fable of common Greek morality. No analogy for human life is as popular as a race, and no tenet is as trite, especially in tragedy, as the warning to judge nothing and no one before the end.[9] Orestes is successful in everything on the first day of the games, surpassing all remembered athletes (689). The crowd called him "blessed" as his name, father, and city were proclaimed. The paedagogue inserts a moral comment of his own: not even a powerful man can escape, when one of the gods injures him (696–97). Then Orestes is killed in the final lap of the race. The tale is thus a warning, whose obvious target is the guilty pair. They are the powerful characters: their wealth and tyranny are continually stressed. But all such good fortune is fragile, especially when the god is at work. The old man hints at the moral, and Aegisthus independently draws the same conclusion as he contemplates what he thinks is the body of Orestes (1466–67):"Zeus, I see the image of that which has fallen not without divine resentment." He is, of course, right; the divine hostility symbolized by Orestes' death has in fact come to Clytemnestra. Still, the message of the story applies to all mortals, and may also serve as a reminder that the end of the play is not necessarily the end of the story.

Orestes dies only in word, not in fact. In this play, however, words are facts. They are effective, first of all, by being believed; but the play emphasizes rather the deceit which makes the deed possible than the deed itself. The killing of Aegisthus is actually outside the play. The truly critical moments are those at which Aegisthus and Clytemnestra pronounce ironic judgments on themselves, as Aegisthus does when he attributes the death of the veiled corpse to divine resentment. Clytemnestra answers the false report of Orestes' death by saying that her son "is well as he is" (791), and Electra calls on the vengeance of the dead man to hear. Clytemnestra congratulates the old man on having at last ended the constant shouting of Electra, but Electra does not fall silent—in the following scene she reaches her resolve to kill Aegisthus and receives a song of praise from the chorus. She in fact conducts the deception which replaces his killing in the action. And this episode is followed by her great lament over the urn. Her feeling is misguided, since Orestes is not dead. Yet once again the lament fulfills its function of joining different worlds. Electra ends her lament by expressing the wish to join Orestes in the "house" of the urn and share with him in death as she did in life (1165–70). At this point Orestes is so moved that the recognition is initiated. What Electra says, despite her ignorance of the true situation, is indirectly fulfilled. [10]

Matricide

In the *Odyssey,* no ambiguity is attached to Orestes' killing of his mother; he is held up as an example for Telemachus to follow. But in the tragedians, the matricide is a central issue. Aeschylus's Orestes is pursued by the Furies until he is at last freed by an Athenian court. His murder is the last act in the terrible history of vengeance and murder within the house of Atreus. The version of Sophocles, however, seems on a first impression to return to the epic view of the matricide as a straightforward success for Orestes. While Euripides' Clytemnestra wins sympathy by admitting that she does not rejoice in what she has done,[11] Sophocles' declares that she is not distressed by the thought (549–50). She celebrates the anniversary of the slaughter of Agamemnon as a holiday (277–81). Not only is she deprived of our sympathy, but her killing precedes that of Aegisthus. When Electra plans to perform the deed alone or with Chrysothemis's aid, Aegisthus only is the victim; she may wish to avoid shocking her sister, but also it is he who must perish to liberate the sisters. She is wicked, but the oppressive power is his.

Still, although no Furies appear at the end, there are Furies in the drama.[12] Electra invokes them, along with other deities (110–18), asking them to send Orestes. She describes her mother as living with Aegisthus and "fearing no Fury" (276). The chorus devotes a stanza of song to predicting the coming of a hidden Fury against the adulterers (488–503). When Orestes and Pylades enter the house to kill, they are called "inescapable hounds" (1388), an image which evokes the Furies. And the guilty pair themselves, as a curse on the house, are called Furies (1080–81). The Furies are thus present, and, like the curse which is also briefly mentioned, they inevitably suggest a cycle of vengeance. If the dead Agamemnon has power, so may the dead Clytemnestra. The Fury is a figure of primitive justice, who pursues the offender without regard for motive.

But there is one oddity about the Furies here: both Electra and the chorus associate them not with the murder, but with the adultery—although nowhere else in classical Greek literature do the Furies punish adultery. Electra and Orestes, however, have committed no sexual crime. The Furies evoked are thus set at a distance from them and the cyclic pattern of crime and punishment. A similar technique is used when that cycle is explicitly invoked, in the debate between Clytemnestra and Electra. Clytemnestra defends her killing of her husband as revenge for the sacrifice of Iphigeneia. The war was undertaken for the sake of Agamemnon's brother Menelaus, who had children of his own. They could have been sacrificed instead. Electra answers on behalf of both her father and her sister (554–55). Agamemnon, she says, killed a stag in the grove of Artemis and boasted of it; the goddess was angry and held the Greeks at Aulis, so that they could neither sail to Troy nor go home, until Iphigeneia was sacrificed. Agamemnon performed the act unwillingly. If indeed justice required Agamemnon's death, the same principle calls for Clytemnestra's (576–83). But this argument is pretense, for vengeance would not demand that Clytemnestra live with her fellow assassin and bear his children.

Electra's argument may appear trivial, and it may seem surprising that she refutes her mother by reciting events of which Clytemnestra probably has direct knowledge, while she herself has only heard of them (565). But the argument over the sacrifice of Iphigeneia is serious. The epic called the *Cypria* told the story of Agamemnon and the deer. Aeschylus's *Agamemnon* omits it, leaving the cause of Artemis's anger ambiguous, but implicitly condemning the Trojan War as an unnecessary slaughter. Electra and her mother seem to be arguing on the basis of different mythologies.[13] They almost belong to different worlds, and it is important that Electra has the last word. Electra argues, moreover, that the laws of the Aeschylean world of her mother demand her death, and she is right. Significantly, Electra claims her mother would die "first" by such rules (583), in effect admitting that if such vengeance is legitimate it would not stop with Clytemnestra. Clytemnestra's version of the story involves her death, but also would provide her with Furies. Electra's version, on the other hand, is in accord with the play's Furies, who punish adultery: the murder of Agamemnon is not separated from the adultery and rejection of Agamemnon's children as the reason for killing Clytemnestra. It recalls the *Odyssey,* where Orestes, repeatedly praised, does not apparently suffer at all for his deed.

Clytemnestra defends herself on Aeschylean rules; Aegisthus also calls up the image of continuing suffering just before his death. As Orestes drives him into the house, he asks why a noble deed should require darkness (1493–94), and to Orestes' reply that he is to die where he killed Agamemnon, he asks whether the house must see both the present and future ills of the descendants of Pelops (1495–98). His impending death may give his words a note of prophetic authority, and the final scene is certainly grim. Electra urges that Aegisthus not be allowed to speak, asking what profit he would have from delay (1483–86). Throughout the play words have proved effective, and Orestes linked language and profit in the prologue (61). And Electra's wish to have the dead Aegisthus given to "such buriers as is proper, out of our sight" (1488–89)—scavenger animals are meant—is chilling. The idea of removing him from sight recalls his own plan to imprison Electra, and refusal of burial can hardly be right. When Orestes in his final words says that all who "go beyond the laws" should be killed, he may be doing what his two victims have done, announcing a rule which can be turned against him and accepting an evil omen. Still, there is no more than a hint of future evil. Further, the hints are hints along Aeschylean lines, and the *Oresteia* has a happy ending to long suffering. Orestes announces after killing his mother that "All is well inside, if Apollo prophesied well" (1424–25). Apollo enjoined a crafty approach to "just slaughter" (36–37). While Euripides actually condemns Apollo's prophecy, Sophocles does no more than hint that the end of his drama may not be the end of the story. And even this is not certain: it is the villains who evoke the Aeschylean story. Orestes and Aegisthus refer to prophetic skill near the play's end (1498–99); but Aegisthus's remark that prophecy is not Orestes' ancestral art does not prove his own hints right. Different characters in this play seem to belong to different versions of the story, and we are not told which is to prevail.

Electra

Electra begins her attack on her mother by insisting that the admission that she murdered Agamemnon is shameful, whether the slaying was just or not (558–60). This argument certainly applies to herself, and she confesses that it does. At the close of her tirade she bids her mother proclaim her bad or shameless or foul-mouthed— at any rate, she does not shame her birth from her mother in being so (605–9). It is evident that the debate between mother and daughter is not a unique event, for both participants make it clear that the complaints of the other have often been repeated. Both this scene and the opening exchanges of the chorus with Electra are typical of Electra's life. These episodes point to the basic tragedy of Electra: her nobility, expressing itself in resistance to her mother and Aegisthus, drives her to shameless behavior. In fighting her mother she comes to resemble her. She prays for her mother's destruction as her mother prays for hers, and although her greater claim to justice renders her sympathetic, nonetheless what we behold in her is a damaged personality.

She is ashamed of her behavior, as she tells the chorus (254), yet defends herself on the grounds that she is under compulsion to act as she does, for no noble woman could endure her situation. Chrysothemis points the paradox. She argues that she must obey the rulers in order to live in freedom (339–40). To be permitted the semblance of freedom she must abandon any attempt at its substance. Electra responds by accusing her of acting as her mother's rather than her father's child (341–42). Electra seems to retain some true freedom in her insistence on free speech; but her freedom is in fact a compulsion born of her nature and her situation. Her shameless behavior is primarily a matter of words: she goes outside the house and shames her family; she insults her mother. Electra insists that this is an inevitable process, as her mother's deeds bring out her own words in a necessity of which she is ashamed (619–21, 624–25). But there is thus a terrible similarity between the deeds of one and the words of the other.

It is for this reason that the recognition is so crucial. Electra's lament over the urn reveals that the hatred which proves her nobility and her shamelessness is not her only feeling. And the recognition is followed by a long passage in which Electra sings joyously as Orestes, in spoken verse, tries to calm her. At last the old man emerges and rebukes them for talking and endangering themselves when they should be concerned with action (just as he stopped Orestes from listening to Electra's opening lament). The theme of Electra's unrestrained speech thus takes a new direction. The recklessness which showed itself in the expression of her hatred for her mother now shows itself in her joy at recovering Orestes and the old man. That the rebuke is needed is important: she cares for her friends more than she thinks of vengeance on her enemies, fierce as she is in assisting in the latter. In the final scene she at last controls her tongue. Instead of being the victim of deception, she becomes its agent, elegantly leading Aegisthus to his death. In her next to last speech she tells Aegisthus that she has, in time, "gained sense, so as to aid the stronger side" (1464–65). In pretending to abandon free speech she wins it. Earlier we heard that Electra could safely come outdoors because Aegisthus was away; in obeying his command to open the gates in silence (1458), she gains freedom from him. Ironically, it is her hypocrisy which truly suggests liberation, for it allows Aegisthus to judge himself. The Electra who sings in joy at the return of Orestes and who is humble before Aegisthus is not the Electra who resembles her mother in abusing her.

The drama's protagonist is Electra, and Electra is truly saved by the outcome, although the play has revealed the terrible cost of her endurance to herself. The final choral tag announces that the children of Atreus have won freedom after much suffering (1508–10). There are hints which suggest that the story may not be completely over. Yet against these hints stands the imagery of the dream. At times Electra and Clytemnestra seem to be setting alternate traditions into contention, as if the issue were whose version will prevail. Even the hints at the darker side do not really affect Electra. Significantly, her last word in the play is "release" (1490). The prophetically threatening words of Aegisthus are addressed only to Orestes, who does not fear evil omens. And even the versions of the myth which send the Furies after Orestes eventually restore him to his home and throne. The triumph of the end is real. The play does not make vengeance pretty. Electra's nobility is not gentle, and she is driven beyond due limits; Orestes is determined to make Aegisthus suffer as much as he can (1504). But the result is just.

Chapter Seven
A Desert Island: *Philoctetes*

The Story

In the "Catalog of Ships" in the *Iliad,* we hear of Philoctetes, an archer who led seven ships to Troy (2. 716–25). He did not reach Troy with the others, however, but lay suffering on Lemnos with a wound given him by a cruel hydra. The Greeks, however, were to remember him before long. Here the complete story of Philoctetes is present in brief. He owned the bow of Heracles, whose arrows were inescapable. But on the way to Troy he was bitten by a serpent during a sacrifice, and the wound festered. The Greeks therefore left him on the island of Lemnos. But when the Trojan prophet Helenus was captured by Odysseus and said that Philoctetes was needed if Troy was to be taken, Diomedes went to Lemnos and brought Philoctetes. The hero was healed by Machaon the physician and killed Paris, whose abduction of Helen was the cause of the war, with his bow.

The story was told in the post-Homeric epic called the *Little Iliad.* It had obvious appeal for the tragedians. Naturally Philoctetes would be resentful toward those who had abandoned him, and their successful persuasion of the sick man had obvious dramatic potential. Aeschylus based a drama on the story. His play included a chorus of Lemnians, who apparently came on their first visit to Philoctetes in all the years he had been on the island. Odysseus came and was, it seems, unrecognized; he won the sympathy of Philoctetes, telling him that his enemies, Odysseus and the sons of Atreus, were dead, and stole the bow during an attack of Philoctetes' illness. Philoctetes came to Troy half-willingly, half-forced. In 431, Euripides produced his *Philoctetes* (along with the surviving *Medea*). A chorus of Lemnians apologized for neglecting Philoctetes, but he did have a Lemnian friend, Actor. Odysseus was accompanied on his mission by Diomedes; Odysseus went unrecognized because Athena had altered his appearance. Odysseus pretended to be a victim of one of his own famous intrigues, the plot against Palamedes, and so won Philoctetes' sympathy. When a Trojan embassy arrived to solicit Philoctetes' help, Odysseus argued the cause of Greek patriotism.[1]

Sophocles' *Philoctetes,* produced in 409, opens with two striking innovations: the drama begins as Odysseus and the young son of Achilles, Neoptolemus, reach Lemnos, an uninhabited island. Neoptolemus, in the epic tradition, was fetched to Troy from his home on the island of Scyros by Odysseus about the same time Philoctetes was brought from Lemnos by Diomedes, and played an important part in the city's capture. Odysseus explains to the young man that he is to lie to Philoctetes. Keeping his true identity, he is to tell Philoctetes that the Greeks refused to give him his father's armor when he came to Troy, and he is sailing home in anger. Winning Philoctetes' trust, he must steal his bow. For he cannot be persuaded to come, and his inescapable arrows make force useless. The young man is unwilling to tell lies, but Odysseus convinces him that Philoctetes' bow is essential to his own promised glory. Odysseus will send a scout if the other seems to tarry. The chorus of Neoptolemus's sailor-followers enters (135) as Odysseus exits, in lyric dialogue with Neoptolemus expressing their eagerness to serve him. They pity Philoctetes, who has lived alone in the cave before them. Neoptolemus says that his sufferings came from the goddess Chryse, at whose altar he was stung, and are the concern of some god, who prevents Troy's capture before the fated time.

Philoctetes enters (219), dragging himself on his wounded foot. Greeting Neoptolemus warmly, he tells him his story, how miserable his life has been since the Greeks abandoned him in his sleep. Neoptolemus tells him that Odysseus and the sons of Atreus robbed him of his father's arms, and the sailors sing how they cried out to the Great Mother to behold the outrage (391–402). As Philoctetes asks about his friends in the Greek camp, it seems that the good have all died, while the evil thrive. Neoptolemus announces his departure, and Philoctetes begs to be taken home to Oeta. The chorus urges him to pity. Philoctetes is about to bid farewell to his cave, when a merchant enters (542). He warns Neoptolemus that the Greeks have sent old Phoenix (Achilles' tutor) and the sons of Theseus to find him. Odysseus was on another errand with Diomedes. Odysseus had captured the prophet Helenus, who said that they could never take Troy unless they persuaded Philoctetes to join them. And Odysseus had promised to bring him, willing or otherwise. The merchant exits, and Philoctetes hastens to gather what he needs from the cave. He tells Neoptolemus he will permit him to handle the bow, and the young man expresses his pleasure in having found a friend who repays kindness. They go within (675), and the chorus sings of the misery of Philoctetes' life, limping on his wounded foot, without bread or wine. Now, however, he will be saved, since he has met a noble friend.

But when the two emerge, Philoctetes has an attack of his illness. He gives Neoptolemus his bow, cries in agony, and at last falls asleep. The chorus urges Neoptolemus to escape now with the bow, but Neoptolemus insists that the bow is useless without the man; the glory must be his. When Philoctetes recovers, he thanks Neoptolemus for waiting, and they prepare to go. But Neoptolemus is increasingly uneasy, and finally admits that he plans to take Philoctetes to Troy (915–16). Philoctetes is enraged, and demands the bow; if it is not returned to him, he will die, a prey to the beasts who have been his prey. Neoptolemus is irresolute, and as he hesitates Odysseus appears (974). At first he threatens to take Philoctetes by force, but then claims that others can wield the bow. He and Neoptolemus go to the ship, but Neoptolemus allows the chorus to remain until preparations for sailing are complete (1074–80). Philoctetes sings a lament, as the chorus insists that his own obstinacy is to blame for his suffering.

But Neoptolemus reenters, followed by Odysseus. The young man is determined to return the bow to Philoctetes, and Odysseus's threats do not move him. Odysseus exits (1257–58) and Neoptolemus calls Philoctetes, who has retreated into his cave. As he hands the bow back, Odysseus reappears (1293–94), and Philoctetes has to be prevented from shooting him by Neoptolemus. After Odysseus's exit (1304), Neoptolemus tries again to persuade Philoctetes to come to Troy, promising him healing and the glory of taking Troy. But Philoctetes can see only evil in joining that evil crew. He asks Neoptolemus to fulfill his promise and take him home, and offers to use his bow to defend him against the Greeks, if need be. As they set out, Heracles appears above (1409) as a messenger from Zeus. First reminding Philoctetes how he himself suffered, but won endless fame, he tells Philoctetes that he is to go to Troy, be healed, kill Paris, and receive the prize for valor. Troy is fated to be taken twice by the bow of Heracles (Heracles himself had once captured Troy). But Philoctetes and Neoptolemus must revere the holy places when they take Troy. Now Philoctetes resists no longer;

he says farewell to his cave and the nymphs of the island, and with Neoptolemus and the chorus goes toward the ships which will convey them to Troy.

Neoptolemus

The introduction of the young Neoptolemus into the story of Philoctetes is a major innovation. The drama becomes his history as well as that of Philoctetes, depicting his heroic education. He must learn to follow his noble nature, his *physis,* and to resist corrupting influence. This aspect of the work is immediately approachable; Neoptolemus's basic character is sympathetically established from the start. He does not want to use deceit, and in this resembles his father, greatest of Greek heroes, who said that he hated like death "the man who says one thing, but hides another in his heart."[2] Desiring glory, however, the young man is vulnerable to Odysseus's persuasion, because the heroic code does not clearly distinguish true excellence from fame. Most of the time a desire for glory is a guide to noble conduct, but in a community whose standards are corrupt it does not provide a basis for opposition. The arguments of Odysseus are not entirely consistent. First he asks Neoptolemus to give himself to Odysseus "for a brief shameless day" (83), with a promise that he can be just another time (82). Later, however, he claims that to tell a lie which brings safety is not shameful at all, and that Neoptolemus, if he succeeds, will be called "wise and good at once" (109, 119). The first arguments cause Neoptolemus to resist on the basis of his nature; Odysseus has admitted that deceit is contrary to his *physis.* But to Neoptolemus's claim that he would prefer a noble failure to a base victory (94–95), he opposes his own greater experience, the lack of alternatives, and his relativist ethic: instead of an admitted wrong to be justified by the delight of success, we hear that the wrong is not wrong. The older man's authority is effective.

The prologue has established Neoptolemus's ethical confusion and the importance to him of his father. Our awareness of his unwillingness to deceive and of his need to imitate his father are crucial to the strangeness of the scenes which follow, until he reveals the truth to Philoctetes. We know that he intends to lie, and he does. Nonetheless, we accept his responses of pity and respect for Philoctetes as genuine. His response to Philoctetes' wondering whether he first should inquire about Neoptolemus's suffering or mourn Achilles is to remark that Philoctetes has griefs enough of his own (339–40). His sincerity is evident. Not only can he not fail to respond to Philoctetes himself, but the lonely man also wins his sympathy by his regret for Achilles. Further, even as he lies he states important truths: even those as clever as Odysseus, he says, are often tripped up (431–32).

The chorus is utterly loyal to Neoptolemus. But the sailors express their pity for Philoctetes even before he enters. Their part in the intrigue is thus somewhat disconcerting, as this genuine feeling then seems to be counterfeited when they urge their chief to accept the pleas of Philoctetes. When he describes how the arms of his father were refused him, they support the lie with an unnecessary song. "There also, Lady Mother, I called upon you" (395), they cry: in making the present address to the goddess a repetition of a prayer which never occurred, they in effect compound a lie with perjury. In the antistrophe which corresponds to this brief song, they speak of avoiding divine wrath by bringing Philoctetes home (517–18). Most strangely, they sing of the homecoming of Philoctetes even when Neoptolemus and Philoctetes are within the cave, so that there is no need to deceive: after reiterating their pity for the long suffering of the hero, they say that now he will be great and happy, having met with the son of a noble family, who is bringing him home (718–29).[3]

The effect of this peculiar steadfastness in deceit, joined with our knowledge that Neoptolemus is unsuited to lying, is to introduce a certain perplexity in the spectator corresponding to the cruel perplexity of Neoptolemus. The intrigue has the same goal, as far as the stage action is concerned, as would the story as Philoctetes sees it. In either case the conclusion must be an exit to the ship of Neoptolemus. So as long as Neoptolemus is not forced to decide what his course will be, we are allowed to drift with him, leaving open the possibility that he will make his lies truth.

The attack of Philoctetes' disease forms a major transition. Neoptolemus is given the bow, which is both his immediate object and a potent symbol of heroic tradition. His prayer on receiving the bow is ambiguous, as he asks the gods for a safe voyage "where the god thinks right and the fleet sails" (780–81). In the previous ode the chorus seemed to express his own inner doubt. Now when the sailors suggest that he seize the opportunity of Philoctetes' helpless sleep to steal away with the bow, he replies that the bow is no use without the man: "the crown is his" (841). The actual goal, Troy, finally reappears; but Neoptolemus now sees both that he cannot win glory by acting without honor and that Philoctetes has real claims of his own. So, fearing to "appear base" (906), and realizing that he has "left his own nature" (902–3), he tells the truth, insisting that he wishes to save Philoctetes from his agony and share the fame of taking Troy with him. But Philoctetes will not be convinced, and the possibility of an easy success, in which Neoptolemus can renounce deceit but profit from it, is gone. Neoptolemus, having underestimated the power of Philoctetes' hatred for the Greeks, confronts a new dilemma. He has "long" felt pity for Philoctetes (966), and is in desperate perplexity when Odysseus appears to reassert his authority. Silent through the following debate between the older men, he leaves the chorus, which in its lyric exchange with Philoctetes resumes the role of speaking for Neoptolemus. The chorus insists that Philoctetes has brought his doom on himself, and that fate, not the members of the chorus, has undone him. Their pleas to him not to reject their friendship are in effect those of the absent Neoptolemus, so that when he refuses to be overcome, the reentry of Neoptolemus with the bow is prepared. He now prefers justice to wisdom (1246, 1251), and has realized that his rejection of his previous shameful course is insufficient if he continues to profit by it; he has to retrieve his mistake (1248–49). Once he does so, the drama of Neoptolemus is over, for he has returned to his best nature.

This nature is, of course, his inheritance from his father. Throughout the play he is continually addressed as "son of Achilles" or as "child" by both Philoctetes and Odysseus. Important to his character is the fact that he never saw his father alive. The significance of the father is marked obliquely in the lie he tells. All we know of earlier tradition about Neoptolemus's arrival in Troy is that Odysseus gave him the famous arms. In Neoptolemus's story, his chief motive for sailing to Troy was his desire to see his father before Achilles' burial, though he mentions the promise that he would take the city (350–53). When he landed, everyone swore they saw Achilles again (357–58). When he demanded the arms of the sons of Atreus, they said they now belonged to Odysseus, and when Neoptolemus burst into tears and cried in protest, Odysseus claimed he had earned them. Neoptolemus then abused Odysseus, who requited, and so Neoptolemus decided to sail home to the island of Scyros. The story is obviously modeled on the quarrel of Agamemnon and Achilles in the *Iliad:* Agamemnon, forced by the anger of Apollo to give up his own prize of honor, decides to take that of Achilles, who bursts into tears. Later he tells the embassy that he will sail home to Phthia, though he never actually does so. The lie, though it is Odysseus's idea, expresses Neoptolemus's essence: he wants to resemble his father.[4] There is a strange pathos in the telling of this tale to Philoctetes—he does not know the story of the *Iliad*. But he immediately asks if Ajax endured the sight of such an injustice, and is told by Neoptolemus that Ajax had already died (410–15). The audience is thus reminded of the quarrel of Ajax and Odysseus for the arms: Neoptolemus has in a sense simply put himself in the place of Ajax.

Arms are always of great symbolic value; they represent the selfhood of the warrior who bears them. Neoptolemus has not literally been robbed of his father's gear, but in being persuaded to violate the *physis* he inherited from his father he is being robbed more deeply. At the same time, the tale represents Odysseus as one who claims the arms of another, and so prefigures the theft of Philoctetes' bow, which Odysseus says he could wield himself (1058–59). Neoptolemus ends his recital by declaring that he blames rather the leaders than Odysseus, for the bad become so by the words of their teachers (385–88). Philoctetes draws a similar moral about Neoptolemus (971–72, 1008–15). Philoctetes responds to the lie as Odysseus hoped he would, comparing the pretended mistreatment of the young man with his own; he claims that Odysseus "would touch every evil word or crime with his speech" (407–8): the judgment best fits neither his own history nor the lie, but the present enterprise.

The lie is made of a mixture of traditional elements which point to central truths; the other important lie, that told by the false merchant, works the same way, putting into a pretended future a variant (the mission of Odysseus and Diomedes) for what is taking place. But through the vagueness of the first part of the play, the lie sets in motion a possible resolution of the action: Neoptolemus takes Philoctetes home. When the bow has been returned to him, so that the Trojan destination seems to have been excluded, Philoctetes argues that Neoptolemus should not want to return to Troy; victimized in the matter of the arms, Neoptolemus should know what the Greeks are like (1363–65).[5] Although the deception has been uncovered, Philoctetes still believes this part of the lie. At this point, the play seems to be moving toward Neoptolemus's fulfillment of his earlier promise to Philoctetes, so that the false direction of the first section would be made true. This possibility, it seems, might almost make the premise of that false direction, the anger of Neoptolemus over the arms, also true. Certainly Neoptolemus does have proof of the power of corruption, which Philoctetes stresses (1360–62), and has nearly been robbed. In Neoptolemus's rebellion against Odysseus, the inner meaning of the lie has been made true. Yet the lie points, above all, to Achilles as the model for his son, and Achilles' abandonment of the Trojan expedition was no more than a threat: in the end he stayed at Troy and died there. Thus the evocation of the lie is a reminder that even a justly angered hero cannot reject the world in which glory can be won.

Odysseus

As an exemplary tale the lie is accurate: the Greek army is a corrupt and corrupting world. Neoptolemus has been made the tool of Odysseus, and Odysseus rightly calls himself the agent of the army. Philoctetes' view of that world is correct. When the chorus urges Neoptolemus to steal the bow while its owner sleeps, the suggestion points to the similarity between the present intrigue and the time, ten years past, when the Greeks abandoned the sleeping Philoctetes. Little has changed, except that many good men have died. Ajax is gone, and Neoptolemus's assertion that Ajax would have prevented the robbery of the arms is a distortion which recalls the real wrong done Ajax (412–13). One item in the catalog is an innovation. When Philoctetes asks about "an unworthy man, but cunning and shrewd-tongued" (439–40), Neoptolemus first thinks of Odysseus (thus revealing what he thinks of his mentor), but replies, once Philoctetes explains that he means Thersites, that he lives. In the epic *Aethiopis,* Achilles killed Thersites, and was ritually purified of the murder by Odysseus.[6] The detail has two effects: it dissociates Achilles and Odysseus, and it marks the complete corruption prevalent in the Greek army for which Odysseus stands.

Odysseus, however, is not a villain of melodrama. He has an ethic of his own, based on the power of language and of change. His exhortation to Neoptolemus to give himself to Odysseus for one brief, shameless day, "and then forever after be called the most pious of men" (83–85), is sincere; for Odysseus time is a series of discrete moments which have no relation to one another. Hence he can say to Philoctetes (1049–51):

Where there is need of such-and-such a kind, I am that kind. Where there is a contest of just and good men, you couldn't get anyone more pious than myself.

For Odysseus there is no continuity in the self, and it can make sense to be a liar today and an honest soul tomorrow. This attitude is diametrically opposed to the belief in an inherited excellence of nature. Indeed, the complete surrender to flux it demands removes the distinction between being and seeming; people are no more than their appearance at any moment. The only standard which stays through time for Odysseus is success. "I am of a nature that seeks victory everywhere" (1052), he says.

But Odysseus, though he doubtless represents a type of politician all too common by this point in the fifth century, is also a servant of Zeus. He is reminiscent of Theramenes, who rose to prominence during the events of 411, and was nicknamed "Buskin," the shoe that fits either foot, because of his shifts of allegiance. Still, he claims divine support for his policy (989–90), and the epiphany of Heracles confirms that this claim is justified. He himself came to Troy under compulsion, tricked out of his feigned madness (1025), but has determined to serve the army. He insists that the journey to Troy will not make Philoctetes a slave, but the equal of the best (997); while he is ruthless compared to Neoptolemus, his evaluation of the most desirable outcome is shared by the son of Achilles, even when the young man is fully disillusioned with him. He is aiding his friends (1145). His views are repugnant, and he teaches that ends justify means: he embodies the corruption of a degenerate world. But his world is the only world in which significant action is possible, and the divinely ordained end does bring him success, even if that is not its purpose. While the drama shows him frustrated and humiliated, it also vindicates his claim to serve Zeus.

The Prophecy

The prophecy which motivates the action is puzzling in several ways. Like other Sophoclean oracles, it varies in different renditions.

One question is crucial: does it demand that Philoctetes must himself come to Troy, or only his bow? If Philoctetes himself must come, must he come willingly? If so, does tricking him meet the condition? One interpretation of the play is based on the idea that Odysseus violates the conditions of the prophecy and is thus impious.[7]

At the opening the plan is left slightly vague, but clearly Neoptolemus is to steal the bow (113) as a preliminary to controlling Philoctetes. Neoptolemus tells the chorus that Philoctetes' sufferings are part of a divine plan to delay Troy's fall until the fated time; his apparent ignorance in the prologue is probably no more than an expository device. Philoctetes must be overcome by craft, because force and persuasion are both impossible. But when we hear more of the prophecy from the false merchant, we are told that Helenus told the Greeks (611–13)

That they would never sack the Trojan citadel, unless, persuading this man with speech, they brought him from the island where he now lives.

Odysseus is then said to have promised to bring Philoctetes whether he was willing or not. Odysseus seems to be contradicting the oracle the moment it is given. The speech is not trustworthy, not only because it is a lie, but in its avoidance of the subjects that might put Philoctetes on his guard: guile and the bow.

When Philoctetes falls asleep, the chorus urges that Neoptolemus escape with the bow. He insists—in dactylic hexameter, meter of epic and oracles—that Philoctetes must come: "His is the crown, him the god said to bring" (841). There is no point in having the chorus suggest something which is out of the question, and Neoptolemus speaks in the tone of one who has come to realize a truth he has not known all along. Yet clearly what is at work in Neoptolemus is not meditations on the prophecy, but Philoctetes. Nonetheless, the false merchant's speech shows the power of language itself we have so often seen in Sophocles. Just as one force that liberates Neoptolemus from Odysseus may be the license Odysseus gives Neoptolemus to abuse him, so the report of the oracle, which may not be intended to be accurate, soon is in accord with the available possibilities. Once Neoptolemus tells the truth, guile is no longer possible, and only force or persuasion can bring Philoctetes—the alternatives of the merchant's speech (593–94), though not its prophecy.

The choice between the bow alone or guile becomes the bow alone or force. Odysseus at first prepares to force Philoctetes (985). But Philoctetes curses him vehemently. In Neoptolemus's lie we heard that Odysseus was roused to anger, though normally cool (377). Now Philoctetes angers him, and he claims that he or Teucer can use the bow as well; he will win the glory that should be Philoctetes' (1055–62). This might be a bluff.[8] Yet there is no reason to think so except a conviction that Odysseus must know the oracle requires that Philoctetes come. And we have not heard the prophecy: we have only a lie and a moment of instinct. We know both emotionally and from the legend that Philoctetes must come, so that the thought of Odysseus's use of the bow is distressing, but we cannot know that it is impossible.

But when Neoptolemus returns the bow, he again evokes the prophecy. The prophecy as reported by the false merchant is now ironically vindicated by the failure of the plot to which he belonged: only true persuasion is now possible. Neoptolemus quotes the prophecy, insisting that Philoctetes must come "willingly, of yourself" (1332), and promising him healing from the sons of Asclepius if he does. He presents the prophecy, moreover, as a necessity. It is not a condition, but what will happen. Evidently, this is not something Neoptolemus has understood all along. But neither is it the result of sudden memory or a sharper attention to the exact wording of the prophecy. It is a prophetic insight into the prophecy which adapts it both to the situation and to the vital human reality.[9] Philoctetes must come willingly both because he cannot be forced and because his nature demands a respect which forbids force or fraud. He must come because his greatness demands that he win glory. The point of the prophecy does not lie in its conditions being scrupulously fulfilled; Odysseus pays not too little attention to the prophecy, but too much. The prophecy is a message from the divine world which receives meaning only on the human plane. The change in the prophecy is akin to the change undergone by the oracle in *Women of Trachis:* as long as the human characters were in a position to steal the bow, it seemed as if this might satisfy the prophecy. Once only persuasion is possible, Neoptolemus cites the prophecy in a form which stresses the need for persuasion. Elegantly, the message was already present in this form in the speech of the false merchant, where the speaker cannot really understand what he is saying, since persuasion is shown in the end to be different from

the deceit in which the merchant is involved. But we must realize
that the shift is not just a trick that keeps the play going by allowing
us to ignore the futility of Odysseus's schemes, nor is it proof of a
failure to understand: the prophecy, like that in *Women of Trachis,*
despite its origin with the gods, is a human message, and develops
only with the mortals who understand it.

Neoptolemus is fully aware both of divine intention and of the
greatness of Philoctetes: what he says is satisfying at every level.
We instinctively demand that the prophecy be fulfilled as strictly
as possible, that Philoctetes win glory and be healed. Yet Neoptolemus fails. In effect, each character blocks one solution: Neoptolemus abandons guile, Odysseus gives up force, and Philoctetes
refuses persuasion, even though Neoptolemus can honestly set not
only his own words but the gods on the side of agreement.[10] Neoptolemus has treated the prophecy's fulfillment as sure, and has framed
it as primarily concerned not with the Greeks but with Philoctetes.
Still, mortals are under no obligation to fulfill prophecies. As the
Greeks were not required to take Troy in the earlier version, so
Philoctetes is not obliged to be healed. But Heracles at last performs
what Jocasta in *Oedipus* said the god would do (724–25), declaring
directly the plans of Zeus. What he says conforms with Neoptolemus's version of the prophecy (he promises Asclepius himself instead of his sons), but he unites the direct word of the gods with
the fullest possible reminder of Philoctetes' essential nature, symbolized by the bow Heracles gave him. Through Heracles, the
process of uniting the divine plan and the man Philoctetes is com-
pleted: in Heracles the prophecy becomes a fate which, imitating
Heracles' own, is fully appropriate.

Philoctetes

The social contract.   In making Lemnos an uninhabited island, Sophocles has not only increased Philoctetes' loneliness, but
put him outside civilization. He lives as fifth-century thinkers imagined early humanity lived—in a cave, sleeping on a bed of leaves,
drinking from a primitive cup, painfully building his fires.[11] All
this we learn even before he appears (27–36). Later he himself defines
shelter and fire as his basic necessities (298–99). A choral song
expands on his lack of grain or wine (706–717), the nourishment
of civilized humanity. He has a primitive medicine; he lives as a

hunter. When the bow is stolen, he sees himself as the prey of the animals he has hunted: as an isolated man, his margin of superiority over the beasts is narrow.

The "Ode on Man" of *Antigone* shows the association in fifth-century thought among domination of animals, agriculture, technological progress, medicine, and political life as elements in human progress. Philoctetes with his simple artifacts is at the very beginning of this development. Since there are no other human beings on the island, he is cut off from that association with others which is essential to being fully human (we may recall the famous definition of man as a political animal which opens Aristotle's *Politics*). Philoctetes has language, but no use for it, and when other humans come at last, they seek only to manipulate him.

In the "Ode on Man" the keeping of oaths is mentioned as a condition of civic existence. In his frustration at Philoctetes' refusal to listen to his advice, Neoptolemus complains that he has "grown wild" (1321), and proceeds to call on Zeus as guardian of oaths to witness the truth of the prophecy (1324). The oath plays a special part in the play. Neoptolemus promises to bring Philoctetes home (527), although when he promises not to leave Philoctetes during his sickness Philoctetes explicitly refrains from exacting an oath. Later, however, the promise becomes an oath in the eyes of Philoctetes (941, 1366, 1398). The promise is not actually an oath, perhaps because it is not fulfilled, and neglect of an oath would be impious even if Philoctetes no longer wished to go home. But it is the equivalent of an oath, and the sanctity of oaths is at the root of human society. Without trust, no community is possible. Thus, when Neoptolemus agrees to make his promise good, he establishes the beginnings of a social contract with Philoctetes—the agreement fifth-century speculation posited as the origin of society.[12] And Philoctetes responds by promising in return to defend Neoptolemus's territory against Greek reprisal. Ironically, it is this agreement which seems to overturn the prophecy through which the fulfillment becomes possible. In accepting the friendship of Neoptolemus and associating himself with another man, Philoctetes effectively rejoins the social world from which he has so long been divided. Only after this symbolic return to society can he actually enter the world of men at Troy.

The bow of Heracles. This friendship between Philoctetes and Neoptolemus is effectively a repetition of that between Philoctetes and Heracles. Friendship is based on the exchange of kindly services. It is the relation to Heracles which above all defines Philoctetes, for he is, above all, the owner of the bow. The bow was Heracles' gift to Philoctetes in return for the service of lighting Heracles' pyre, and it symbolizes both excellence and friendship. Hence when Philoctetes first tells Neoptolemus that he may handle the bow, he reminds the young man that he received it in return for a benefaction (670), and Neoptolemus responds with an expression of his pleasure at thus obtaining a friend who returns good for good. So he accepts that earlier friendship as the model for his own. The choral ode which follows amplifies the theme. The song begins by comparing the sufferings of Philoctetes to those of Ixion. Ixion, punished in Hades for his ingratitude to Zeus, is the moral opposite of Philoctetes, and the opening thus poses a question about divine justice. But the song's end concerns Philoctetes' return to his home at Oeta, "where the bronze-shielded hero drew near the gods, shining in the divine fire of his father" (727–29). The words hint at the part Philoctetes played while suggesting, through the reference to the apotheosis of Heracles, that the gods do reward men.

Thus the agreement between Neoptolemus and Philoctetes is more even than the creation of a new society; it is at the same time the re-creation of a heroic tradition which is a special concern to the gods. Heracles, through his labors (1418–20), won deathless glory. The achievement of Philoctetes is to echo that of Heracles (who once took Troy); fate decrees his bow must take Troy twice (1439–40). The direct link with the gods is stressed by Heracles' promise to send Asclepius, the healing god himself, to heal Philoctetes (1437). Heracles likewise emphasizes the closeness of Neoptolemus and Philoctetes, who are to be like lions in a pride (1434–37). The appearance of Heracles is not a concession to the mythical tradition which demands that Philoctetes reach Troy at last.[13] The alliance of the young warrior and the old leads naturally to the epiphany of the figure who stands before them in the heroic line. Despite the corruption of the world in which their triumph is to take place, Heracles' epiphany gives that triumph real meaning. The two form a better society unto themselves, in which their deeds have their place, and at the same time the gods provide a fuller and eternal context.

Yet the play does not end on a note of complete blessing. Heracles reminds the pair to be reverent in all that pertains to the gods when they sack the land (1440–41). "For piety does not die with mortals; it does not perish for them, living and dead" (1443–44), are his last words. The entire drama has linked excellence, justice, and piety; what Neoptolemus had to learn is that success has no glory without justice and piety. Now Heracles actually speaks of an immortal piety which echoes the eternal glory he has won. The warning is a reminder of the infamous impiety of Neoptolemus at the sack of Troy, when he butchered old Priam at the altar of Zeus. Although the happy fate of Philoctetes, destined to win glory and return home safely, dominates the conclusion, we are reminded that the heroic society so painfully re-created in the drama was extremely fragile. Neoptolemus will again be corrupted. Philoctetes, the isolated sufferer, will again be isolated as the only representative of a just and pious glory.

Chapter Eight

Time Defeated:
Oedipus at Colonus

Plot

Oedipus, an old, blind beggar, asks Antigone, his daughter and guide, where they have come (an outline of the family of Oedipus can be found at the opening of chapter 3). She replies that they are at some distance from a city—Athens—and apparently in a sacred grove. A passerby warns them to leave the place (36–37): they are trespassing on holy ground, sacred to the Dread Goddesses, the Eumenides (another name for the Furies). Oedipus prays that they receive him graciously as their suppliant, for he will never depart from this land. Their name marks his fate. Oedipus asks for further information, and learns that the area is Colonus, and it is ruled by the Athenian king, Theseus. Oedipus asks that a messenger tell Theseus that he is offered a great benefit in return for small help. The stranger exits to report to the local people, and Oedipus prays to the Dread Goddesses to have thought for himself and Apollo, who promised that here, at a shrine of the Dread Ones, he would find rest from his troubles. Hospitably received, in death he would help those who received him while injuring those who drove him out. A sign from Zeus would mark the fulfillment of all this. Now Antigone sees the chorus of old men of Colonus approach, and the pair hide themselves in the grove (111–16).

The old men search for the violator of the holy ground, and Oedipus comes forth, indicating his blindness. Expressing pity, the chorus urges him to leave the ground where it is not lawful to walk in order that they may speak to him. With Antigone's encouragement, Oedipus, in the course of a lyric dialogue, is slowly led by Antigone to a seat of natural rock beyond the holy limits, having obtained a promise from the chorus that he will not be driven away. But they question him about his identity, and, again with Antigone's encouragement, he admits that he is Oedipus (222). The old

104

men cry that he must leave. They were tricked into an unfair promise, and they fear he carries a curse. Antigone appeals to their pity,
and Oedipus reproaches them with fearing no more than a name,
disproving their city's fame for her piety toward suppliants. He was
morally innocent. The old men agree to allow Theseus to judge.

Ismene arrives with news from Thebes (324). The earlier decision
of Oedipus's sons not to seek the throne has been put aside, and a
god and their own wickedness have driven them to rivalry. Eteocles
has exiled Polynices, who has gone to Argos to gather allies for an
attack on Thebes. And new oracles give Oedipus power over the
welfare of Thebes; Creon will try to settle him somewhere under
Theban control, but—for fear of pollution—outside the borders.
If his tomb does not receive their offerings, his wrath will afflict
them someday. Despite this oracle, the brothers did not try to bring
their father home. Oedipus prays that the gods not put out their
fated strife, but put its outcome in his power, so that neither succeed.
He was exiled from Thebes only when he had lost the desire to be,
and his sons made no attempt to help him. But the strangers will
win a savior if they defend him. The chorus suggests that he make
an offering to atone for his trespass. The rite, a series of libations,
is described, and Oedipus sends Ismene to perform the ritual on his
behalf.

In lyric dialogue (510–48), Oedipus yields to the request of the
chorus to tell his story. Theseus enters. Reared in exile, he understands the vicissitudes of mortal life. Oedipus explains that his body
is his gift, and explains the aims of Thebes. Theseus, surprised at
this apparent promise that Oedipus will help defeat Thebans on
Attic soil, wonders how trouble could arise between the Thebans
and himself. Oedipus speaks of how all things change in time:
someday the Thebans will break the peace for a small cause, and
his cold corpse will drink their warm blood. Oedipus wants to stay
at Colonus, the fated place, but warns that aggressors will come.
Theseus, confident that his power will be a sufficient deterrent,
exits (667).

The chorus sings in praise of Colonus: the grove with its flowers
and nightingales, haunted by Dionysus, the water of the River
Cephisus, the love of the Muses and Aphrodite for the place. The
olive tree flourishes here, and Poseidon has given the inhabitants
mastery of horses and the sea. Antigone warns that the land must
prove its praise: Creon is coming (720–21). He enters with an armed

guard, but speaks graciously, asking Oedipus to return home. Oedipus replies that he seeks to be kind only when his kindness is not wanted, and in any case Creon is lying about his plans. Cursing Thebes, he prays that his sons have enough land there to die in. When he orders Creon to leave, Creon reveals that he has captured Ismene. He now has Antigone seized. The guards take her away; when the old men try to hold Creon, he threatens to take Oedipus also. Oedipus prays that Creon's old age be as bitter as his own. Theseus enters (887), brought from a sacrifice to Poseidon by the noise. Sending a detachment to recover the girls, he warns Creon that he will be held until they are safe. Athens is a city of law.

Creon answers that he did not think Athens would interfere with his just claims on his own family, or that the pious city would receive an incestuous parricide. Again Oedipus defends himself, and blames Creon for speaking of his family's shame. Taking Creon with him, Theseus goes in pursuit of the abducted girls (1043). A choral ode imagines the coming battle.

The chorus's prayers for victory are instantly answered as the maidens enter with Theseus and attendants. Theseus declines to boast of the battle, but tells Oedipus that a suppliant from Argos is sitting at the altar of Poseidon. Recognizing Polynices, Oedipus has to be persuaded by Antigone to see him. The chorus sings of the cruelty of old age: best not to be born, second best to die young. Oedipus is like a cape on a wind-beaten shore, pounded by waves on all sides. Polynices enters (1254) weeping and regretting his bad treatment of his father. Oedipus is silent. Polynices tells how he has been unjustly driven out, and asks that Oedipus leave his anger: the side he joins will win. Again Oedipus is silent; when the chorus bids him speak, he curses his sons: they will slay each other. Antigone tries to convince her brother to give up the expedition, but he cannot endure the shame of deserting. He blesses his sisters, and begs them to care for his burial, if the curse is fulfilled. After his exit, a clap of thunder breaks into the choral song (1456). Oedipus asks that someone bring Theseus.

When Theseus arrives, Oedipus says that his end has come. He will guide Theseus to the appointed place, but Theseus must tell no one but his heir, to protect his city. All the actors exit, led by Oedipus (1555), and the chorus sings a prayer that his death be gentle. A messenger enters (1579), and tells the old men how the blind man led them. He said an affectionate good-bye to his daughters, saying that his love requited all they had done for him. A voice cried from above, "Oedipus, why are we waiting?" and Oedipus, commending his children to Theseus, sent them and the attendants away. And when they looked back, Oedipus had disappeared, as Theseus made reverent gestures to both earth and sky. Antigone and Ismene enter (1668–69) and sing a lament with the chorus. Theseus returns. He forbids Antigone to seek her father's grave, but grants the request of the sisters to be sent back to Thebes to try to prevent the coming war. The chorus ends by calling for an end to lamentation, "for these events have authority."

Sophocles did not invent the legend; there is a passing allusion to it in Euripides' *Phoenician Women* (1705–7).[1] Probably, however, he was the first to make the story of Oedipus's death at Colonus the subject of a literary work. The play is the latest of his surviving works, and probably the last actually composed; it was produced only after the poet's death. Colonus was his deme, and therefore in all likelihood his home. When the stranger at the opening of the play has listed the divinities of Colonus for Oedipus, he concludes (62–63): "Such are these places, stranger—not honored in words, but more in living with them." The play enacts how Oedipus enters among these local sanctities. The probably very simple local legend is made a drama through its ready adaption to an established kind of tragedy, the suppliant play.

Athens and Thebes

The earliest surviving example of the subgenre modern scholars call the suppliant play is the *Suppliant Women* of Aeschylus. Two more pure examples survive from Euripides, *Suppliant Women* (not the same as Aeschylus's) and *Children of Heracles*, while several other tragedies contain elements of suppliant plot.[2] Suppliancy is an essential social mechanism of archaic Greek life, the only protection available for the helpless in a world little governed by law. A suppliant places himself under divine auspices so as to demand protection from other human beings. To reject one who performs the ritual is to risk the anger of the gods, especially Zeus, one of whose titles is Protector of Suppliants. In the suppliant play, a suppliant or group of suppliants comes to the place where the drama is set and takes refuge at an altar. When the political leader of the place asks what they seek, he learns that they are not mere refugees, but are actively persecuted by their enemies, who will demand that they be given up, or for some other reason require military help. Thus he and his people must decide whether to accept the suppliant. Refusal is impious and may bring the anger of the gods, but acceptance brings a more immediate threat. The issue may be complicated by the suppliants' not being entirely praiseworthy: Aeschylus's Danaids seem to reject marriage (they are pursued by their cousins, who seek to marry them), while Euripides' suppliant women are the mothers of the Seven against Thebes, who undertook a war though omens from the gods showed they were doomed to fail. But the suppliant is accepted, and the persecutors first threaten and then attempt force. Good prevails.

This plot has an inherent moral, serving to praise the civic order which defends the helpless. All but one of our suppliant plays are set in Attica, and it was a special pride to Athenians to consider their city the defense of the weak; Oedipus alludes, anachronistically, to this reputation in our play (260–62). Such drama had an obvious appeal for Athenian patriotism, and this one was composed during the dark days of the last part of the Peloponnesian War, when Colonus, near the city as it was, was exposed to Spartan raids.[3] The suppliant plot, however, does not consist in mere vulgar self-praise. The idealized Athens of the play is not only a depiction of how Athens imagined herself, but an example of the true self she should strive to be. The true encomium reveals to its subject the excellence possible in himself. Oedipus, received in Attica, provides a military protection; the play, depicting the process of his reception, not only justifies this gift of the gods but reminds the recipients of the merits by which they earned it.

The stages by which the suppliant is accepted are in this work complex. Although we are first directed to expect the arrival of Theseus, who alone can officially accept Oedipus, very early (70), he does not enter until 551. Two factors complicate the reception of Oedipus: his trespassing into the grove and then his horror-provoking identity. The Stranger's first words are a warning to leave the holy soil (36–37), and the issue is elaborated by the entry-song of the chorus. The old men imagine that the trespasser is the "most unrestrained" of human beings (120). When Oedipus finally leaves the holy space, the importance of the theme is marked by his slow and difficult passage across the acting space. This first obstacle is overcome easily. But the holy ground is a refuge as well as a barrier.

Once he has entered the profane realm, he is threatened by the second danger, his name. The parallelism between his decision to leave the grove and that to declare his name is marked by his turning for advice to Antigone both times (170, 217), and he admits his identity only because he relies on the promise he extracted from the chorus on leaving the holy ground. This first segment concludes when the chorus, moved by Antigone's plea and Oedipus's arguments, agrees to wait. Oedipus has claimed to be "holy, pious, and bringing a benefit to the citizens" (287–88).

Ismene brings oracles which confirm Oedipus's claims, and Oedipus, in repeating his promise to the chorus, exhorts the elders to join the goddesses in defending him (457–60). Now the chorus calls Oedipus and the maidens "worthy of pity," and he answers by addressing the chorus-leader as "dear friend" (465). The elders now urge Oedipus to atone for the trespass, and offer detailed instructions on how he is to do so. The instructions conclude with the statement that the chorus would have courage to stand by Oedipus if the rite is performed, but would be afraid for him otherwise (490–92). Earlier the old men were afraid of the name which evoked the terrible curses attached to parricide and incest, but now they seem willing to defend Oedipus, as long as the rite is performed. In each case there is an offense against the Furies. The trespass into the grove and the crimes of Oedipus are thematically linked; the ignorant wandering onto land where it is forbidden to go re-creates the crimes committed in ignorance, evoking especially the incest.[4] But in Attica the Furies are called Eumenides, Kindly Ones, and the name is employed in the prayer dictated by the chorus (486). In this context the careful attention given each ritual action is not just local color. Rather the details, charming and gentle as they are, emphasize the sense of reconciliation.

Ismene is sent to perform the ritual: "One suffices in making this atonement for many, if he is present with goodwill, I think" (498–99), according to Oedipus. Ismene's exit is followed by lyric dialogue in which Oedipus reemphasizes his moral innocence; he married his mother "knowing nothing" and killed his father in self-defense. The ritual averts the anger of the Furies, while the dialogue asserts his innocence so as to avert the revulsion of humanity from his crimes. Pollution was a taint which attached itself to actions without regard for the intent behind them, and Aeschylus's Furies in *Eumenides* insisted that no rite of purification could wash away the blood of a parent. In becoming the Eumenides of Athenian cult, however, they were absorbed into a legal system in which the pollution of crime could be removed ritually, while guilt could be judged in a court of law. The trespass into the grove would not cause pollution, but the atonement is treated as assuaging the wrath of the Eumenides. By the time Theseus arrives, the obstacles to the reception of Oedipus have been overcome. The elders' fears have been calmed.

Theseus accepts Oedipus without hesitation, offering his help even before Oedipus promises him any benefit, on the grounds of the traditional morality which reminds all mortals of their shared vulnerability. So the motif of the city's fear to receive the suppliant is exploited in an original way, as a clash of piety with piety. At the same time, the city, in the person of the king who is its ideal representative, accepts its obligation to the suppliant without question and earns its reputation.

Even so, the chorus can still wonder if the thunder which calls Oedipus to his death is a sign of divine wrath (1483–84). At Thebes the fear of Oedipus as a carrier of evil is dominant, and is the reason for their plan to settle Oedipus nearby. In the debate between Creon and Oedipus before Theseus, Creon claims that he meant no disrespect to Athens, but assumed Athenian piety would reject Oedipus (944–46):

I knew that you would not receive a parricide, an impure man—not one who was discovered sharing an impious marriage of parent and child.

He assumes that Athens thinks—or can be led to think—as Thebes does. Oedipus's reply employs themes he did not use with the chorus, predestination by the oracle and the possible curse. He stresses his own lack of evil intent with Creon's voluntary abusive behavior. These arguments, while they do support his moral innocence, might also suggest that Oedipus is hated by the gods who caused his crimes, and might best for safety's sake be avoided. The debate underlines how Theseus chooses a humane over a merely ritual piety.

The Thebans' piety makes Oedipus an object; their wish to control, but not accept, him enrages Oedipus. Indeed, Creon implicitly admits the wrongness of this scheme when he first addresses Oedipus, by pretending that he comes to bring Oedipus home (741, 757–58)—a pretense Oedipus angrily refutes in his response (785–

86), while promising that Thebes will have his avenging spirit instead. To fear too much a curse carried by Oedipus is to receive one. Athens is rewarded because her conception of piety is generous. It is not without concern for ritual, but its gods accept ritual repayment for accidental transgressions. Creon and the Thebans join concern for a narrow piety with a willingness to lie and manipulate. But the Athenians learn to disregard the "mere name" of Oedipus in favor of their tradition of compassion. The repeated harangues of Oedipus are integral to the action, for in this case it is the horror evoked by Oedipus's deeds, not an external threat, which provides the tension in the suppliant plot.

Oedipus the Hero

The drama is a struggle for control of the powers of the dead Oedipus, which will benefit some and harm others. The power to help or hurt is characteristic of the hero, *hērōs* (already briefly discussed in connection with *Ajax*).[5] Heroes were dead men who exerted special power, especially near their graves or other relics, and they were prominent in classical Greek religious life. While most of those we think of as Greek "heroes"—the characters of epic—were honored with hero-cults, there were many heroes (and heroines) who were figures only of local legend or had no legend at all. Indeed, many were anonymous. The discovery of a Bronze Age tomb could easily prompt the establishment of a hero-cult. Legends tell of heroes first honored by the directive of an oracle, in response to a city's question about the cause of a plague or other calamity: a hero could be dangerous if neglected. An extraordinary death could bring about a cult—a man who mysteriously disappeared, or was struck by lightning—and sometimes historical persons received worship as heroes after their deaths.

Often heroes had cults subsidiary to those of major gods; the hero Pelops was buried in the precinct of Zeus at Olympia, Neoptolemus in that of Apollo at Delphi. While the exact location of Oedipus's tomb is not revealed in the play, he is closely associated with the goddesses; the other shrine of Oedipus in Attica was inside the precinct of the Eumenides on the Areopagus (Pausanias 1.28.6–7). As a hero's power was so closely connected with his remains, both legends and history present examples of the transfer of the bones of a hero from one place to another (Pausanias in the second century

A.D., not believing Sophocles' account of the death of Oedipus, thought his bones had been brought to Attica). Struggles over a hero's bones are not surprising. What is extraordinary is that the struggle over the hero Oedipus takes place while he is still alive. All the tragedies of Sophocles are studies in the meeting of human and divine will: here the theme is explicit.

The dead Oedipus will have great power, but he will not be in control of it. The rules governing the event are mechanical. If the Theban plot succeeded, Oedipus's wrath after death would be averted. The Thebans, having his grave under their control, would make proper offerings (libations of blood were the main offering to heroes), and apparently Oedipus would not be able to avoid being propitiated. His power, once established by his death, is not directed by his personal will. Nor will he be conscious to enjoy it. His pleasure is in the anticipation of receiving the blood offering—when his cold corpse will drink his enemies' blood (622). Hence he and the gods are agreed as to what the results of the play's action should be. Apollo, according to the oracle Oedipus cites as soon as he hears of the presence of the goddesses, promised him rest in such a spot, with the ability to help those who received him and hurt those who cast him out. Thus it would seem that his death at Colonus is already forecast, so that attempts to change this fate are doomed to fail. But Oedipus himself takes the threat from Thebes entirely seriously. Furthermore, Apollo's oracle was a prediction, not a command, and mortals have no obligation to assist a god in fulfilling his prediction. Hence the emotional response of Oedipus to Ismene's report of the Theban plan is critical. If Oedipus's sons had been loyal to him, or the Thebans been willing to accept him in their land, he might have returned willingly. What Oedipus will do as hero is already announced in the prologue, yet it is also determined in the course of the action, by the gods with their oracles, by the Thebans and Athenians, and by Oedipus.

Posterior Justification

Although Oedipus dominates the drama, remaining on stage from the beginning until he finally goes out to his death, it is a mistake to see the play as exclusively about Oedipus himself.[6] He is a static figure. His future power as a hero is a given, not really a goal toward which he works. The drama of the play is derived not from the protagonist, but from the opposing sides who contend for him. Their relative fates are announced in advance. Nonetheless, their futures do not seem to be predetermined; Oedipus can change them. The contending sides in each case help seal the fate that Oedipus has already promised. At the same time, the actions of characters justify the blessing or curse Oedipus has already decreed. Poetic justice, or complete reciprocity, prevails. This is clearest in the relation of Oedipus with Athens. His initial citation of the oracle, which makes Colonus the destined place, means that Athens is to be the beneficiary of Oedipus's death, if the city accepts him. When Theseus receives Oedipus without any concern for what Oedipus can give him in return, he not only obtains the blessing, but earns it.

The words which mark the reciprocity of Oedipus's dealings are *kratos* ("power") and *soteria* ("salvation"). Ismene tells Oedipus the Thebans will need Oedipus "for the sake of their salvation" and because he will have "power" over them (390, 392). Only a few lines later, the Thebans are said to want to obtain "power" of Oedipus without admitting him to their soil (400). Shortly thereafter Oedipus calls himself a *soter* ("savior") for the Athenians (460, 463). The prayer enjoined by the chorus is that the goddesses receive the suppliant "for salvation" (487), with a surely deliberate ambiguity; Oedipus asks the chorus for "salvation" from Creon (725), and Theseus "saves" Oedipus's daughters. The Athenians save Oedipus, and are rewarded with the "salvation" Oedipus can provide in the future. The Thebans seek "power" over him, and their return is his "power" over them.

The Theban and Athenian actions toward Oedipus are clearly typical of the respective cities. The Theban scheme is, in effect, a repetition of the original exile of Oedipus, which came not when in his anguish after the discovery of his crimes he wished to be cast out, but later, when his grief was calm (431–41, 761–82). The oracle of *Oedipus the King*, requiring his exile to end the plague, is not mentioned in this play. In the dispute with Creon, Oedipus compares the behavior of Thebes in the present with the past: then they cast him out only when he no longer wished to go, while now they seek to bring him home (at this point he pretends to believe Creon's promise of a return to Thebes) when another city has received him kindly, and he no longer needs care. The relationship of friendship between Oedipus and Athens, on the other hand, is something new, although it is based on the Athenian custom of protecting suppliants. It is, however, intended to be eternal, as Theseus passes the secret of the place of Oedipus's burial to his heir and he in turn to his. The Athenians are forced to defend Oedipus with military power, and in return he will someday help them defeat Thebes in battle.

Oedipus consciously lives by a rule of reciprocity.[7] The chorus first invokes the principle of returning like for like, claiming that as Oedipus deceived the elders in obtaining their promise of not disturbing him under false pretenses, they are justified in ignoring the promise (228–29). Oedipus then invokes the rule in defending himself: he killed his father in self-defense, responding to attack, and so would have been innocent even had he known the other's identity (271–72). For Oedipus, even the relation between father and son does not affect the fundamental return that good is returned for good, evil for evil, although Antigone denies that extension of the rule in pleading for Polynices (1189–90). She invokes the benevolent side of the principle when she reminds Oedipus that he owes kindness to Theseus and herself, and should not refuse their plea (1201–3).

Polynices tries to use the similarity of situation between his father and himself to evoke Oedipus's sympathy: both are beggars and exiles (1335–37). Too late he sees how he neglected to care for his father (1264–66). To the argument from similarity Oedipus makes no reply. In fact, Oedipus's potential of heroic power effaces the resemblance; he, unlike his son, does not live by "flattering" others (1336), and the dramatic situation reveals how Oedipus differs from Polynices, for Oedipus, a suppliant at the opening of the play, now receives his son as his suppliant. The only reciprocity between father and son is the justice of Oedipus, which curses both his sons for their failure to maintain him.

Oedipus repeatedly intertwines his sons and the city of Thebes. Both fall under his curse, and receive within the action of the drama destinies which at the same time seem already theirs. That of Thebes is mentioned in the prologue, while Oedipus's first reference to their quarrel is a prayer that the gods not quench their "fated" strife (421–22). We first hear of their neglect of their father as a contrast with their sisters (337–45), but soon after their offense is linked with that of the Thebans. They neither opposed his original exile, nor have they used the recent oracle to press for his return, preferring to contend for the kingship (418–19, 441–44). The old man's tirade modulates easily between his sons and the city. Again in his angry speech to Creon, after he refutes Creon's hypocrisy, he makes a double return: for the Thebans, his avenging spirit in the land, and to his sons enough Theban soil to die in (786–90). In each case, his curse is a neat inversion of the benefit his enemies seek. But the children and the city are intertwined at a deeper level also. The curse against the sons, that they possess enough Theban soil to die in, recalls the city's offense against Oedipus, that of wanting to control his grave without allowing him burial in Theban ground. The Thebans, on the other hand, are punished by Oedipus's death in a foreign land, so that they will be unable to care for his grave and must suffer from his angry spirit. This recalls not only the Thebans' own crime, but that of Oedipus's sons, since caring for their father was more their special obligation than that of the city. This pattern does not contradict the peculiar appropriateness of the fate Oedipus gives each of those he curses, but reveals how close they are to each other.

The sons of Oedipus show how the decrees of Oedipus are carried out and justified by others. The strife of the brothers is fated, and Ismene attributes it to both "someone of the gods and their wicked mind." Oedipus asks of the gods that the issue be in his hands. In the following episode, Oedipus suggests that the gods may have an ancient grudge against his family (964–65). He prays that his sons receive enough Theban land to die in. When Polynices approaches his father, he says that oracles have declared that the victor will be he whose side Oedipus joins (1331–32); Oedipus's prayer has been answered. The great curse of Oedipus includes a proem in which he points out that, had it not been for the help of his daughters, he would have died, so that Polynices is morally his father's murderer (1360–66). The superficial parallelism Polynices drew between his life and his father's thus becomes much deeper: both are parricides. The parallel implies that the curse on the house is upon Polynices and his brother. The final curse then echoes this theme, as he prays to the Furies and the nether gods to cause Polynices to die by a kindred hand and to kill him who drove him out (1387–89). The curse is linked with the history of the family, but is repeated by Oedipus. But in the following dialogue of Polynices and Antigone, it is clear that he understands the curse and expects it to be fulfilled, yet Antigone cannot dissuade him from the expedition. It would be shameful to flee, and Eteocles would laugh at him (1422–23). Polynices agrees to his own ruin, and accepts the curse. This is the crucial moment in its fulfillment; it is justified because Polynices is depraved enough to go consciously forward to fratricide.

The brothers are continually linked with Thebes, but also continually contrasted with their sisters. An echo of Herodotus compares the brothers to Egyptians, who invert Greek norms of male and female behavior (337–60; Herodotus 2. 35). The sisters have kept their father alive, and offer a standard of filial piety by which their brothers can be judged (1360–69, 1379). They also receive a recompense appropriate to them, though it is, as their father admits, a single word (1617–18): "For there is no one from whom you have had more love than from me." The single word "love" repays all the toil his daughters have endured for him. All through the play we have seen the power of a single word. The chorus fears the mere name of Oedipus, while Theseus expects his name alone to deter an assault on Oedipus (667). Oedipus insists that his name does not correspond to his moral self, while Theseus is forced to substantiate his name with force. But Eteocles and Polynices are said to have failed to speak the "small word" that would have prevented their father's exile (443). In contrast to the mere names, which do not have real power, the "small word" neglected by the sons is essentially the same word with which Oedipus rewards his daughters. His love for them is a return equal to any service; where the word which would express this relationship is lacking, the mechanical rules of reciprocity apply.

The offenses Oedipus requites are repetitions in the present of sins already committed, just as his curses are reiterations of propecies already pronounced. Only the reception of Oedipus by Athens is new, and even that is performed in part through a reenactment of his crime through the trespass on the grove. The action of the play compresses time in creating its patterns, and Oedipus's speech on the nature of time and change is at the heart of the play. Theseus is perplexed by the promise that Oedipus, dead, will help Athens to defeat Thebes, because his relations with Thebes have always been good. Oedipus explains that things change, except for the gods (611–13):

Trust dies, mistrust grows; the spirit has never been fixed the same among friends, nor between cities.

Ironically, the prediction Oedipus gives for a remote future is fulfilled within the play. Oedipus himself is the cause of dispute between Thebes and Athens, and the dispute is settled in a battle which both guarantees the result of the future contest and foreshadows it. Time is contracted, and its power of change manifested. Yet there is a deeper irony than this. The relationship of friendship between Oedipus and Athens is to be eternal. The action moves toward the overcoming of the destroying power of time through the death of Oedipus. Once Oedipus dies in Attica, his grave saved from Theban interference by the secrecy of its location, the reciprocities which have been established are fixed. Oedipus becomes a hero, not a god, and the other side of the relationship is a city and its kings, changing from generation to generation. But divine protection saves the friendship between the savior-pariah and the recipients of suppliants. On his way to his death, Oedipus passes the monument of the eternal friendship of Theseus and Perithous (1593–94): this eternal friendship is not quite unique. It seems to be a special dispensation given Athens, or Colonus itself.

The End of the Play

Critics have sometimes tended to treat this play as if it consisted primarily only of its beginning and its end, with the episodes inserted as filler.[8] For this reason it is vital to realize that the drama concerns not a reconciliation of Oedipus with the gods through a miracle, but the working of that miracle in the human context. But the temptation to treat the play this way is understandable, because its conclusion is so overpowering. At one and the same time it points beyond human experience toward divine mysteries and addresses the most universal human experience, for Oedipus weeps with his daughters and is called by a voice from heaven. The thunder and lightning which mark the fated moment raise the tone to one of awe, and Oedipus guides his daughters and Theseus at his exit, in a striking and strange reversal of his earlier helplessness. After this solemn departure, the chorus prays for a peaceful end for Oedipus; the song is a reminder of the pains of Oedipus's life, but one which assimilates him to other mortals. The messenger speech evokes once again the sacred topography of Colonus through which Oedipus moves calmly to his end. In his farewell to his daughters, he claims that their labors for him have been recompensed by his love, and weeps with them. Oedipus has been a fierce and terrifying man, who has suffered terribly, and we feel the experience of long life behind his words. The moment of human intimacy is broken by a voice from heaven—"Why are we delaying?"—(1627–28) whose colloquial tone is more haunting than solemn speech could be. And after Oedipus's disappearance, Theseus salutes both heaven and earth, so that we do not know how Oedipus was taken away.

The conclusion thus unites the deepest human emotions with something supernatural; the death of Oedipus is miraculous, and suited to his uniqueness in pain, yet it also seems exemplary, speaking to the essential of the human condition. It is even more moving because we know it is the work of a very old man. The great song on the evils of old age (1211–48) includes both the choral singers and Oedipus as sufferers; but its catalog of pains—"envy, factional strife, contention, battles, murders"—evokes late fifth-century Athens as much as the world of the play, and we suspect some identification of the author with his character.

The death of Oedipus transports us to a boundary between the divine and human worlds. After his death, the drama returns to the purely human level, marked by Antigone's grief-stricken desire to see her father's tomb (1756–57). Theseus's reminder that the location of the tomb is secret underscores the division between Oedipus as human being and as hero. When the divine purpose is fulfilled, the characters must continue to live under the dispensation the play has created. So the play ends with Antigone's request that she and Ismene be sent back to Thebes. Polynices has already asked that his sisters bury him, if need be (1408–10), so that the end recalls the events of *Antigone* (though not perhaps exactly: Ismene is included in Polynices' request, and this play has shown the sisters as equally dedicated). Oedipus has cursed Creon with the wish that his old age be like his own (869–70). Further suffering is in store, and Oedipus's power to reciprocate good done him will not help his daughters. The girls embody faithful affection, and have been rewarded with their father's love, but this same loyalty will be their ruin. Throughout Oedipus has cooperated with the curse and the purposes of the gods, and these are still at work after his death. But the curse and the divine purpose work to poetic justice only in connection with Oedipus himself. The girls' service to their brother involves them in the curse despite their innocence. The death of

Oedipus hints at reconciliation and perhaps significance in his long suffering, but this hint looks outside the human world of history and tragedy. The other characters continue in mortal time.

Chapter Nine
The Sophoclean Achievement

The Lost Plays

The seven surviving plays show a remarkable consistency of style, and we may fairly assume that in many respects our corpus is typical: the pungent, unusual Greek, the pervasive irony, the use of contrast to create character. But to judge a dramatist from so small a selection of his work—probably a selection made for schools in the second century A.D.—is likely to mislead. We cannot be certain how many plays Sophocles wrote, but are told of 24 victories and 123 dramas. Our information about lost plays varies greatly from item to item. For some we have no more than a title, and since some ancient plays had alternate titles, that does not even prove the existence of a separate work. For others papyri have provided fairly extensive fragments. We have enough knowledge, at least, to put the extant plays in some context, especially that of Sophocles' choice of myths on which to base the plots of his works.

First, the three plays on the family of Oedipus, a striking group among the surviving plays, do not stand out in the corpus as a whole. There were no other works on this family, though several plays dealt with the expedition of the Seven against Thebes and its aftermath—*Alcmaeon, Eriphyle, Epigoni,* and the satyr-play *Amphiareus. Ajax,* on the other hand, is not isolated in the corpus as a whole, for Sophocles composed an *Eurysaces* on an unknown story concerning the son of Ajax, and a *Teucer,* which dealt with the misfortunes of Ajax's brother, whose father cast him out in anger at Ajax's death—events anticipated in *Ajax* (1003–21). There was a *Philoctetes at Troy,* and *Electra* was not the only treatment of the house of Atreus, for Sophocles composed an *Iphigenia* and a *Thyestes,* as well as an *Oenomaus,* which treated the tale handled allusively in song at *Electra* 505ff.

Many lyrics refer to myths on which entire plays were based. The story of Cleopatra (*Antigone* 966–87) may have been clearer to the original audience if they were familiar with his *Drummers* or one of two called *Phineus*. *Electra* 147–49 alludes to the nightingale who mourns the son, Itys, she killed in vengeance on her husband. Sophocles dramatized this story, probably giving it a Dionysiac coloring, in his *Tereus*. Both Antigone (823–38) and Electra (150–52) compare themselves to Niobe. She boasted that she had more children than Leto, mother of Apollo and Artemis; the two gods killed her children, and she became petrified in grief. In a scene of Sophocles' *Niobe* reconstructed from papyri, the two gods stand on the stage building with their attention away from the audience, toward an inner courtyard of Niobe's palace which is invisible to us.[2] Apollo points out to his sister the daughters of Niobe as they try to hide in rooms off around the courtyard, and she shoots them with calm efficiency. Our sympathy for the victims is all the greater because we perceive them through the remarks of the attacking gods; the scene is theatrically brilliant and theologically disturbing.

The surviving titles indicate a wide range. Sophocles probably composed at least one connected trilogy in the Aeschylean manner, a *Telepheia* based on the many adventures of this son of Heracles. For some titles, a happy ending seems almost certain—*Danae, Andromeda*, one of the two called *Tyro*. There were works on specifically Attic legends—the early *Triptolemus*, about the Eleusinian sent by Demeter to teach the world agriculture, *Creusa*, about an Athenian princess's recovery of her exposed son, born after she was raped by Apollo, and *Phaedra*, in which Theseus's wife, convinced that Theseus had died when he disappeared on his ill-fated journey to Hades, succumbed to her passion for her stepson, Hippolytus.

One particular mythological area stands out, however—the Epic Cycle. Sophocles' favorite theme was the Trojan War, its antecedents and aftermath. Odysseus alone was the central figure of a number of works: *Mad Odysseus*, in which he tried to escape the Trojan expedition by pretending insanity; *Palamedes*, where he contrived the judicial murder of an innocent rival in the army; *Nausicaa* or *Washerwomen*, which followed Homer's *Odyssey* for the story of Odysseus's rescue by the princess and their not-quite-romance. According to Sophocles' biography, Sophocles himself played Nausicaa, and was popular in the scene in which Nausicaa played catch with her maids. In *Fellow-Banqueters* (perhaps a satyr-play?), he probably quarreled with Achilles, and in one of the surviving fragments describes how someone threw a chamber pot at his head. In *Spartan Women* he undertook a spying expedition into Troy. Other plays followed the fortunes of Trojans, like *Alexander* (another name for Paris), another story of a foundling restored, *Troilus*, a young prince killed by Achilles, and *Laocoon*, the priest who tried to prevent the Trojans from accepting the Wooden Horse and was killed by serpents sent by the gods. *Eurypylus* has yielded papyrus fragments. Eurypylus was Priam's nephew, and Priam bribed his sister to send her son to aid the Trojans; he was slain by Neoptolemus. A surviving fragment (210 Radt) describes Priam's grief. In *Sinon*, the protagonist pretended to be a fugitive from the Greeks in order to persuade the Trojans to accept the Wooden Horse. They were duped. Another play told the story of Antenor and his sons; when Odysseus and Menelaus came to Troy as envoys to demand the return of Helen, Antenor and his family gave them protection, and were the only Trojans spared when the city was taken. *Locrian Ajax* probably concerned the Lesser Ajax's impiety in dragging Cassandra from Athena's temple; the goddess appeared in the play (fr. 10c). *Polyxena*, about a Trojan princess sacrificed to Achilles, included an appearance of the hero's ghost (fr. 523).

This almost random selection can only hint at Sophocles' versatility and breadth of sympathy. The plots seem to have been of every kind. *Thamyris*, about a singer who boasted of being a finer musician than the Muses, and *Niobe* were stories of sin against the gods and the gods' terrible vengeance, but *Sinon* probably belonged with *Electra, Women of Trachis,* and *Philoctetes* in its fascination with deceit and intrigue. There were plays of *eros*, revenge, and recognition. The special place given stories of the Cycle shows Sophocles' affinity with Homer, for the simplest reason for preferring these subjects is that they allowed him to treat Homeric characters, settings, and themes without entering into direct competition. Furthermore, the Trojan story was the richest single body of Greek mythology. Sophocles' tragedies, unlike the greatest masterpieces of his predecessor Aeschylus, are self-contained. He did not usually compose connected trilogies, and groups like the Theban plays should not be treated as belonging together. But perhaps for this very reason, he set his works firmly within the context of broader stories. All Sophoclean tragedies refer to the past and hint at the future in a way that makes it clear that the story dramatized is only one of many possible stories. Each is complete, but only because art creates a sense of completion. The Trojan War was the ideal source for the kind of story that appealed to Sophocles, where both the complete fate of an individual and the place of the story in a larger narrative could be seen. Moreover, the Trojan War was an event of great complexity, in which Homer had shown sympathy and understanding for opposing sides. Sophocles likewise gave equal attention to Greeks and Trojans. His repeated treatments of Odysseus exemplify one feature of this complex sympathy. Odysseus is not exactly the same personality from play to play, as we can see from *Ajax* and *Philoctetes,* but he has certain characteristics which cannot alter—cleverness, flexibility. In *Ajax* his willingness to change is sympathetic, in *Philoctetes* it is not. The dramas use similar moral contrasts, but the precise qualities stressed completely change our responses. Sophocles' frequent returns to the Cycle for material must have given him many opportunities for this ethical re-vision.

Each group of tragedies presented was followed by a satyr-play, a short and lighthearted piece with a chorus of satyrs, lecherous and drunken part-animal followers of Dionysus. No satyr-play of Sophocles has survived complete, but a significant part of *Trackers* has been rediscovered on papyrus.[3] Like many satyr-plays—Sophocles wrote a *Baby Heracles* and *Baby Dionysus*—this treated a god's infancy, in this case that of Hermes, as told in the Homeric *Hymn to Hermes.* This poem told how Hermes on the day he was born invented the lyre, then stole Apollo's cattle, and finally was reconciled with his older brother Apollo, giving him the lyre. At the beginning of the preserved portion of Sophocles' play, Apollo is announcing a reward for whoever can find his cattle. Silenus, leader of the satyrs, takes up the offer, and the satyrs find cattle tracks. But they lead nowhere (the clever Hermes disguised the trail with false shoes on the cattle's feet). The satyrs are frightened by a strange sound. Silenus mocks them, but when he hears it, he wants to run away. Instead they follow it to a cave entrance (the central stage door), kick, and are answered by Cyllene, nymph of Mt. Cyllene in Arcadia, where the play is set. She explains that she is nursing a new son of Zeus by the nymph Maia, who is still sick from childbirth. The baby is only six days old. There is a riddling description of the lyre, which is finally explained, and the papyrus breaks off as nymph and satyrs argue over Hermes' guilt.

This passage is amusing and has considerable charm, but it is not uproariously funny. The language (as with all satyr-play) is closer to the dignity of tragedy than to the freedom of comedy. Sophocles seems to have used the Cycle as a favored source for satyr-plays as for tragedies, with *Strife* probably treating the quarrel among Hera, Athena, and Aphrodite over the golden apple marked "for the fairest," and *Judgment* giving an allegorizing version of the Judgment of Paris. Other titles include *Hybris, Blame,* and *Lovers of Achilles*—the last is a tantalizing loss, for a chorus of satyr-suitors of Achilles was probably a very funny invention.

Survival

Sophocles wrote and produced in the fifth century B.C.; the first printed edition was published at Venice in 1502.[4] For 1900 years the seven extant plays survived in manuscript. While the precise details of the transmission are difficult to uncover, and interesting only to specialists, every reader should have a sense of the long history behind the text so easily purchased in paperback or checked out of a library. In Sophocles' time, the book trade was primitive. Copies of tragedies doubtless circulated among the author's friends, and admirers borrowed and recopied plays or passages. By the end of the fifth century professional copyist-booksellers seem to have existed. In the following century, original tragedy, though still produced, declined in quality, and after 386 B.C. the dramatic festival included revivals of old tragedies. The masterpieces of the previous century were thus alive on the stage as well as in writing. But this liveliness had its own dangers. Around 330 B.C. Lycurgus, a leading Athenian statesman, regulated performance by requiring actors to follow an official text deposited in state archives in order to prevent them from interfering with the dramas they produced.

This official Athenian version is probably a source of the tradition we inherit. Our Sophocles is descended from that created by Alexandrian scholars in the third and second centuries B.C., associated with the famous library. Ptolemy Euergetes (ca. 280–221) borrowed the official Athenian copy and never returned it (he had a deluxe copy of it made for the Athenians instead). With this and doubtless other copies as a basis, the Alexandrians (Aristophanes of Byzantium did the most famous work on tragedy) edited the plays. Their work produced commentaries, traces of which sometimes appear in the scholia, marginal notes in surviving manuscripts. The early papyri show that lyric passages in drama were normally written as prose; Aristophanes determined their metrical form and wrote them accordingly. He gathered information about the original production

(Aristotle had made this task easier by collecting the records, *Didascaliae*) and gave each play a brief prefatory note.

Sophocles, though second in popularity to Euripides, continued to be read in the Roman world. At some time in the second century A.D. or later, a school edition of seven tragedies was written; Aeschylus and Euripides were likewise excerpted. The disappearance of works not chosen was not as swift or dramatic as was once thought. But learning and pagan literature faded. The plays not selected were not copied, and even the selection fell into long neglect. About 800 A.D. the adoption of a new style of Greek writing (miniscule), had a funnel effect on the tradition. Only those copies of a text which were used in transcribing books into the new script henceforth contributed to the tradition. In the case of Sophocles, it is reasonably sure that more than one old (uncial) manuscript was used, although it is disputed whether there was more than one actual transcription. Our oldest surviving manuscript of Sophocles, the Laurentian (now in Florence) was written in the tenth century A.D. Interest in Greek poetry revived in this period, and Sophocles was repeatedly copied. Later in the Byzantine period he again became an object of scholarly interest. When Greek manuscripts began to be brought to the West, Sophocles was among them. The famous collector Aurispa brought a manuscript of the three plays most popular in Byzantium to Italy in 1413, and a complete manuscript in 1424. In 1502 Aldus Manutius published the first printed text, and new editions have not ceased to appear since then.

Modern Influence

A full study of the influence of Sophocles on modern literature has yet to be written. The task would be immense, touching on the histories of scholarship, reading, and education. Much influence is indirect, and often hard to pinpoint exactly: many writers have been inspired by "Greek poetry" or "Greek tragedy" as a whole, and the place of Sophocles would not be easy to identify. While works which use explicitly Sophoclean themes are not hard to find, often those where Sophocles has been used less obviously have used him more profoundly.[5]

Roughly, the history of Sophocles' dramas can be divided into five main sections: the Renaissance, neoclassicism, German neo-Hellenism, the Victorian period, and the modern period created by the anthropological study of tragedy, Nietzsche, and Freud. While this grouping is, of course, an extreme oversimplification, it defines the main developments in English, French, and German literature. In the Renaissance, although printing had saved the poet from the danger of disappearance, he was not a significant influence on most practicing tragedians. Renaissance Italian tragedy followed the Latin tragedian, Seneca. There was some interest in Sophocles: a free prose translation of *Electra* into Spanish in 1528, and a performance of *Antigone* in Italian in 1532. In the middle of the sixteenth century, the French scholar Jean Dorat lectured on Greek tragedy at Paris, and editions of Sophocles appeared at Paris in 1532–33 (Turnebus) and at Geneva, at the famous Stephanus press, in 1568. The German, Lutheran scholar Melanchthon included tragedy in his popular teaching at Wittenberg after 1518. But the first writer of the first rank to know Sophocles well and be deeply influenced by him was John Milton. The attempt to re-create Greek tragedy in Christian form is explicit in *Samson Agonistes* (published 1671, date of composition uncertain), but Sophoclean echoes can be found throughout Milton.

French neoclassical tragedy was produced in direct emulation of Greek and in a context of debate about the relative superiority of ancient and modern literature. Tragedy was seen through the window of Horace's *Ars Poetica* and Aristotle's *Poetics,* which were seen as laying down normative rules. Racine never adapted a Sophoclean plot, but knew Sophocles well and noted in his texts Sophocles' skill at opening his dramas.[6] His older contemporary, Corneille, produced an *Oedipe* in 1659 (he probably derived his knowledge of Sophocles' play from the Latin translation in the Stephanus edition, and also used Seneca's imitation of Sophocles). The play is typical of its author in its emphasis on duty and resignation: Oedipus consoles himself with the memory of noble deeds and the knowledge that the gods were responsible for his crimes, while his virtues were his own. Despite the neoclassical emphasis on the unity of plot, Corneille's play is diffuse compared with Sophocles', for he introduces a new character, Dirce, daughter of Laius, who brings with her both a love-interest and a political theme. In 1718, the young Voltaire published an *Oedipe* with a polemical preface attacking both Sophocles and Corneille. He objected to what seemed to him failures in plausibility and dramatic construction in Sophocles: the discrepancy in the number of murderers, Oedipus' slowness in seeing the truth, the lack of a final proof that Oedipus is the killer of Laius, the continuation of the play after the revelation. Voltaire avoids most of the problems he identified, but his play is an elegant machine, without dramatic force. He clearly shows what Sophocles meant to neoclassical drama—an example of technique, to be imitated or surpassed. In England, John Dryden and Nathaniel Lee produced their *Oedipus* in 1678, and it was long a favorite on the stage. The piece is a bizarre mélange of elements taken from Sophocles and from a number of Shakespeare's plays, with a sensationalism and prurience entirely its own, strangely charming in its extravagance and lack of taste. Sophocles' play, in one scene almost literally translated, is simply a source of material.

A new and very different Sophocles was to emerge from German Hellenism.[7] In 1755 Johann Winckelmann published the first of his studies of Greek art. Through his influential works Greek art came to be seen as a unity with Greek poetry, so that Sophocles stood with classical sculpture as the ideal of serene beauty, "noble simplicity and quiet greatness." Not everyone accepted the image of Sophocles as an author of radiant calm. Lessing in his *Laokoon* (1766) analyzed the *Philoctetes* in detail to show that it did not offer a calm, resigned attitude to suffering. He insisted that Greek tragedy was true tragedy and therefore aroused and purged pity and fear, unlike French neoclassical drama, which was cold and intellectual. The two points of view differ, but not perhaps radically. Schiller composed a well-known epigram mocking those who could see *Oedipus the King* as serene—"Oedipus tears out his eyes, Jocasta hangs herself, / Both innocent: the piece reaches a harmonious conclusion"—but saw in Sophocles, and tried to imitate, a cathartic balance of emotions. A. W. Schlegel, in his enormously influential *Lectures on Dramatic Art and Literature* (1809), placed him above Aeschylus in all but boldness, and put him far above Euripides. He praised Sophocles for "sweetness and grace," and his brother Friedrich spoke of Sophocles' union of the gifts of Dionysus, Apollo, and Athena and of the excellence of his characterization. Friedrich Hölderlin, one of the greatest of lyric poets, dazzled by his faith in the gods of Greece and his vision of a Germany transformed into Hellas, composed brilliant and eccentric translations of Sophocles. One of his epigrams speaks of the Joy which others tried to speak joyfully, but Sophocles alone expressed through sorrow. And, of course, Goethe studied Sophocles. Though he never composed a work on a Sopho-

clean subject, his reading of Sophocles was influential in the poetic
version of *Iphigenie auf Tauris* and his attempt to compose gener-
alized, Greek-style tragedy in *Die natürliche Tochter.*

Although there were wide variations in the "German" Sophocles,
he can be given a rough general characterization: noble and beautiful,
simple and true to nature, Sophocles' art was defined as a perfect
balance. Certain qualities we might look for today are certainly
lacking. It is significant that A. W. Schlegel liked least *Women of
Trachis,* with its despair about the gods and its eroticism. Still, this
Sophocles was a living and vital poet with great emotional power.
Goethe thought that it was preposterous that the decorous Corneille
pretended to imitate Sophocles; he and his contemporaries looked
to the Greek not for a formal example sanctified by theory, but
with excitement.

The idealized Greece created in Germany formed a prominent
element in nineteenth-century English literature.[8] Schlegel's *Lectures,* translated in 1815, were very influential. Sophocles was important, much praised, read in schools, but perhaps rather dull. He
was seen as a teacher of traditional piety, so that Christians could
make him almost one of their own, while those who had lost faith
could take comfort from him. But a Victorian's loss of faith was
not the joyous paganism sometimes set free in German Hellenism;
in Matthew Arnold, its most famous victim, it was deadly earnest.
Though in *Culture and Anarchy* Arnold defines Hellenism, which
Sophocles should embody, as the striving for "sweetness and light,"
the Sophocles of "Dover Beach," who compared human misery to
the sea (*Antigone* 586–92), is a sad figure, and evoking him makes
the speaker sadder: Dover Beach is "distant" from Greece—the
pagan world is as remote as the retreating Sea of Faith. In "To a
Friend," Sophocles does appear as a real comfort to Arnold in a dark
time; that he "Saw life steadily and saw it whole" seems to have
been real consolation, for which Arnold thanks him. But there is
something melancholy in Arnold's Sophocles—envy, perhaps—and
he is in danger of being boring. It is not inspiring to call a tragedian
one whom "Business could not make dull, nor passion wild."

But Arnold's is not the only Sophocles of the nineteenth and early
twentieth century. At one end of a spectrum, one might place
Shelley's satire *Oedipus Tyrannus: or Swellfoot the Tyrant* (1819), in
which George IV appears in an opening tableau as a fat monarch
supplicated by a chorus of oppressed pigs. At another is E. M.

Forster's *The Longest Journey* (1907), in which Mr. Jackson, whose joy is the reconstruction of lost Sophoclean plays, surely speaks for Forster: " 'Is it worth it?' he cried. 'Had we better be planting potatoes?' And then: 'We had: but this is second best.' " And in between, George Eliot deserves mention in particular for the use made of *Antigone* in *Middlemarch*. Although at the beginning of the book Dorothea is compared to St. Teresa, she is called "a Christian Antigone" later, and the names of both Teresa and Antigone appear at the close. Significantly, Dorothea wants to learn Greek and Latin, and not only for her husband's sake. The classics represent a whole world of male endeavor; George Eliot writes here as a woman who has achieved her character's frustrated ambition. Antigone is a feminist symbol, and was used in this way also by Virginia Woolf, another woman whose desire for equality meant learning Greek and reading Sophocles.[9] Although Sophocles was a "safe" and orthodox writer, he was open to use by rebels and outsiders, including homosexuals, women, and radicals.

The treatment of Sophocles as the preacher of "sweetness and light" was naturally fated to be overturned. Friedrich Nietzsche wrote *The Birth of Tragedy* in 1870–71, defining tragedy as a musical experience in which a Dionysian, irrational, emotional spirit was clothed in an Apollonian form. The anthropology of Sir James Frazer *(The Golden Bough)* inspired a series of studies which treated Greek tragedy as the sophisticated remnant of primitive ritual surrounding the death and rebirth of the Year-Spirit.[10] In 1900 Sigmund Freud published *The Interpretation of Dreams*. The Freudian Oedipus complex gave *Oedipus the King* a peculiar and privileged status. Taken together, the new influences made it impossible for sensitive readers to ignore the darkness and violence of Sophocles' vision. At the same time, tragedy's high claims and grandeur make it an ideal vehicle for the characteristic self-irony of modern writers.

Andre Gide's *Oedipe* (1931) and Jean Cocteau's *La Machine Infernale* (1934) share a view of Oedipus and Jocasta as sexually attracted to each other by their unconscious relationship, and deliberately bourgeois and unheroic features. Gide makes Tiresias a scolding pedagogue, and Cocteau has Oedipus not defeat the Sphinx, but be spared by her because she is attracted to him. The most famous of recent adaptations of Sophocles, Jean Anouilh's *Antigone* (1944), constantly depends on its original for the full effect of its prosaic manner and for the equivalent of a sense of fate. Characters speak of their "roles," which seem predetermined because Sophocles has predetermined them. Hugo von Hofmannstahl's *Elektra* (1903), well-known in a slightly shortened form as a Richard Strauss opera, lacks this type of irony, but shares with Gide's and Cocteau's adaptations a concern with the characters' psychology.

The works and authors I have mentioned are barely a fraction of those who might have been discussed, especially in recent times. While relatively few people nowadays read Greek, the flood of translations is unceasing; Welsh and Bulgarian have recently received translations of Sophocles. The volume of critical literature also continually increases, and the mutual influence of critical reinterpretation and literary revision can only be expected to continue.

Omissions and Generalizations

One of the uses of a survey of readings of an author is to inspire humility in the interpreter. Sophocles has been made what his readers wanted of him, and my reading may be no exception. Still, there are elements which unite all treatments of the poet. I have not stressed his great central protagonists in this study, because they have been the center of attention of much Sophoclean criticism in English for the past thirty years, and because no reader or member of a theater audience needs to have the grandeur pointed out. The Sophoclean protagonist is a lonely figure, isolated from society by his or her insistence on extremes. Antigone and Electra refuse to accept the limitations on action established by Greek sexual norms. Ajax refuses to accept a world of change and compromise; Philoctetes refuses to participate in the corruption of the Greek camp. Oedipus will not hold back from learning the truth. Deianeira, who does not refuse society, but dies trying to keep her place in it as Heracles' wife, is perhaps the loneliest of all.

Against these figures stands a chorus, which typically sympathizes with the protagonist but does not share his sense of how imperative his ethical demands must be. There are two main types of Sophoclean chorus. Those of *Ajax, Women of Trachis, Electra,* and *Philoctetes* are closely linked with a single character, and present a sympathetic background of his situation. The chorus composed of elders, on the other hand, has more independence. In *Ajax* and *Women of Trachis,* where the action continues after the deaths of Ajax and Deianeira, the chorus falls silent. In *Antigone,* however, the chorus stands apart from both Antigone and Creon. In *Oedipus the King,* the dramatist has deliberately avoided using the chorus for his suppliants in the opening scene; the chorus members are loyal to Oedipus, but are not ethically dependent on him. In *Oedipus at Colonus,* the chorus is hostile to the protagonist and must be won over. Both types of chorus serve to contrast the loneliness of the protagonist and leading characters like Creon and Neoptolemus with their own social presence. Both add depth to the dramas by presenting mythical antecedents and analogies. The chorus of elders is the singer of the great Sophoclean songs, where there seem to be innumerable layers of superimposed irony and references to many characters at once, like the "Ode on Man" (*Antigone* 331–75) and the Second Stasimon of *Oedipus the King* (863–910). These songs reach a level of moral generality at which we cannot help but feel that they must be true, but are faced with many complexities in relating them to the plays in which they stand. They are relevant, but do not provide easy morals. In these songs the chorus seems partly to shed its individual personality and become a neutral, choral voice, with all the traditional authority of choral poetry.

Sophocles' dramaturgy developed throughout the portion of his career represented by the extant plays, becoming gradually more fluid. In the earlier plays characters tend to make their decisions offstage and announce them when they appear, while in the later plays we see their hesitation and choice. Corresponding to this greater flexibility of characterization is a less rigidly formal use of other elements. Choral entries are songs exchanged with actors instead of purely choral songs. Lines are more often divided between two actors in excited conversation. Many features, however, persist through many works. Characterization by contrast, most notable in *Antigone* and *Electra,* is used throughout. The rare props carry great symbolic weight: the sword in *Ajax,* the urn in *Electra,* the bow in *Philoctetes.* So do places in several plays—the hostile soil of Troy in *Ajax,* the desert island of Lemnos in *Philoctetes,* the holy Colonus of *Oedipus at Colonus.* Certain dramatic tricks appear repeatedly: the joyful song before a report of catastrophe (*Oedipus the King, Ajax, Antigone, Women of Trachis*) the silent exit portending a suicide (Jocasta, Eurydice), the prayer to a statue of Apollo beside the door apparently answered by the entry of a messenger (*Oedipus the King, Electra*). There is little hesitation in depicting horror: Heracles and Philoctetes suffer agonizing physical pain on stage, Oedipus appears with his ravaged eyes. Sophocles is not usually thought of as a contriver of spectacle, but Heracles appears from the machine in *Philoctetes,* and there were probably sound effects for the miraculous thunder of *Oedipus at Colonus,* while *Ajax* comes closer than any other tragedy to making the audience witnesses of violent death.

Outstanding in all Sophoclean drama is its intensity. There are relatively few characters, and these do not have the psychological depth found in the characters of novels or in Shakespeare's plays, or for that matter in Euripides. Character is tightly bound to action, but at the same time action is always expressive of character. The characters are reduced to essentials, and we learn exactly as much as we need to feel emotionally involved and to understand action. Complexity is offered not by the close depiction of inner forces, but by the network created by various facets of character and situation: thus Antigone is both doing what is right and carrying out the curse on her family. It is inherent in her situation that she has reasons not to regret death, but as a young, unmarried woman should especially regret it. All these aspects are presented. Typically a Sophoclean drama involves great complexity of causality combined with clearly drawn character and a few, highly significant actions. The plays are filled with references to time, and the actions of the plays serve to summarize entire lives. Echoes of the past and foreshadowings of the future meet so that what happens is a culmination of what has been and a determinant of what will be.

Much of the machinery involves conventions we no longer share, aspects of Sophocles' world which no longer have meaning. The plays are crammed with oracles and curses, and the gods are omnipresent. These features should not be ignored, or made into rationalized modern equivalents, for one of our best reasons for continuing to read and perform these works is their mixture of strangeness and accessibility. Oedipus's insistence on knowing the truth communicates itself to us, despite the way this truth is embedded in oracles, and so does Philoctetes' disgust at the corruption of his heroic society, although we do not share his heroic values. When we accept the Sophoclean world on its own terms, we can feel the power of human beings who act in concert with divinities. Divine-human interaction is one of main elements of this theater, and moderns can feel the awe of this relationship without completely understanding it.

Many of the recurring themes are familiar to us. The difficulty in finding the truth experienced by Oedipus and Deianeira, the destructive power of erotic passion shown in *Women of Trachis* and *Antigone,* the assault on the personality of long loneliness in a Philoctetes or an Electra—all these speak to moderns directly. Above all, Sophocles can still offer a peculiar, often painful satisfaction in the union of "authority" and simplicity of action with complexity and difficulty. It is never easy to know exactly why things have happened as they do; causes are many, depending on multiple human relationships and on the unknowable purposes of the gods. At the same time, we see the causes combine in such a way that the results seem inevitable, and what happens is somehow what must happen. In this way the plays do not preach or offer easy meanings, but insist that the actions they represent have meaning. At once satisfying, disturbing, and frightening, the Sophoclean world seems inexhaustible.

Notes and References

Chapter One

1. This bare sketch inevitably distorts much that is complex and controversial; the reader should consult such standard works as J. B. Bury, *A History of Greece,* 3d ed. (New York: St. Martin's, 1951) or N. G. L. Hammond, *A History of Greece to 332 B.C.* (Oxford: Oxford University Press, 1967).

2. On the festivals and the technicalities of classical performance, see A. Pickard-Cambridge, *The Dramatic Festivals of Athens,* 2d ed. (Oxford: Oxford University Press, 1968). There is a fine brief introduction to the theater in O. Taplin, *Greek Tragedy in Action* (Berkeley: University of California Press, 1978), pp. 1–21.

3. On the structure of tragedy see the work of Taplin cited in the preceding note. In referring to the choral personality, I do not distinguish between lines spoken by the chorus-leader alone and songs sung by the group; my use of the singular for "the chorus" and the plural for "the elders" or the like does not reflect any difference in how the chorus is actually working in any passage.

4. Aristotle, *Poetics,* 1449a.

5. All the evidence for Sophocles' life is collected in Radt, *Fragmenta,* pp. 29–95 ("Testimonia," abbr. T). The biography itself is translated in M. Lefkowitz, *The Lives of the Greek Poets* (London: Duckworth, 1981), pp. 160–63 (discussion of the biography pp. 75–87). The anecdotes from Ion of Chios survive in the *Deipnosophists* of Athenaeus (13.603E ff.). Other interesting anecdotes survive in Plutarch (*Life of Cimon* 8.7 and *Life of Pericles* 8.5).

6. See V. Ehrenberg, *Sophocles and Pericles* (Oxford, 1954), pp. 120–36.

7. This story is open to some doubt. Many poets' legends include cultic elements. Sophocles was famous for his piety, and his paean to Asclepius (fr. 737, PMG) connected him with that god. His last play concerned a hero, Oedipus, and poets were often imagined to have prophesied their own fates. Thus, there is a basis on which the story could have been invented. The hero Dexion certainly existed; inscriptions of the third century B.C. attest to his worship. His identification with Sophocles, however, is possibly a later fiction.

8. Aristotle, *Rhetoric,* 1419a 25.

9. An excellent introduction to these issues is W. K. C. Guthrie, *The Sophists* (Cambridge: Cambridge University Press, 1971; reprint of *A History of Greek Philosophy* (1969), vol. 3, pt. 1).

Chapter Two

1. *Little Iliad*, fr. 2.
2. *Nemean* 7. 24–30; 8. 22–27.
3. P. 106 15–23, *Aethiopis* fr. 2, *Ilias Parva* frs. 2, 3 Allen; (English translation) pp. 509, 513 Evelyn-White for the *Cycle*.
4. *Iliad*, 17. 645–57. Apparently Ajax's burial was a source of contention already in epic. One known detail of Aeschylus's treatment is interesting: Ajax was invulnerable, and the messenger who describes his suicide says that a goddess helped him find the spot where he could be wounded (fr. 292 Mette, 41 Smyth).
5. Ajax probably appeared on the *eccyclema*, a wheeled platform used to display interiors, but the use of this device in the fifth century is controversial.
6. Teucer, subject of another Sophoclean play (frs. 576–79, Radt), was forced to leave home, and founded the city of Salamis on Cyprus.
7. See G. M. Kirkwood, "Homer and Sophocles' *Ajax*," *Classical Drama and its Influence*, ed. M. J. Anderson (London, 1963), pp. 51–70.
8. The emphasis given these lines and the messenger-speech divides "orthodox" critics from "hero-worshippers": a brilliant "orthodox" treatment is that of R. I. Winnington-Ingram, *Sophocles, an Interpretation* (Cambridge, 1980), pp. 12–13, 40–41—his Ajax is a megalomaniac even when sane; on the other side, critics such as R. Lattimore, *The Poetry of Greek Tragedy* (Baltimore: Johns Hopkins, 1958), pp. 72–74, stress the lack of integration of the *hybris*-theme into the play.
9. So the ancient commentator (scholiast) on 1123: "Trying to make the drama longer he became insipid and lost the tragic emotion."
10. The best introduction to hero-cult is still E. Rohde, *Psyche*, trans. W. B. Hilles (1925; reprint ed., New York: Harper and Row, 1966), pp. 115–55. I am especially indebted to P. H. Burian, "Supplication and hero cult in Sophocles' *Ajax*," *Greek, Roman, and Byzantine Studies* 13 (1972):151–56.
11. The complexity of who protects whom may have been increased by the fact that Eurysaces himself had a shrine in Athens (Pausanias 1.35.3 and inscriptions of the fourth century B.C.); he was the subject of a Sophoclean tragedy whose plot is unknown (223 Radt, the only fragment, is a single word).
12. Commentators differ on Athena's invisibility. Odysseus says (14–17) that he easily knows her voice *even when* he does not see her; I do not

see the point of this if she is visible to him. Nonetheless she should be standing close to him (I compare *Iliad,* 2. 172–83).

13. Fairly close to my opinion is O. Taplin, "Yielding to Forethought: Sophocles' Ajax," in *Arktouros: Hellenic Studies presented to Bernard M. W. Knox* (Berlin: de Gruyter, 1979), pp. 122–30, but he sees as Ajax' conscious decision what I see as intuition. For a very different interpretation, see B. Knox, "The *Ajax* of Sophocles," in *Word and Action: Essays on the Ancient Theater* (Baltimore: Johns Hopkins, 1979). (This essay was first published in 1961.) 125–60.

14. Twice in the *Iliad* (16. 852–54; 22. 358–60) characters have a prophetic gift at death; Socrates refers to the phenomenon in the *Apologies* of both Plato (39C) and Xenophon (30).

Chapter Three

1. There is some difficulty over who speaks these lines (manuscripts do not have authority on the identity of speakers); editors and commentators differ. But it is surely the chorus which is addressed, not, as has been suggested, Iole.

2. A good bibliography and review of the issue is T. Hoey, "The Date of the *Trachiniae,*" *Phoenix* 33 (1979):210–32, though I am not convinced by the author's arguments. The fullest treatment is E.-R. Schwinge, *Die Stellung der Trachinierinnen im Werk des Sophokles, Hypomnemata* 1 (Göttingen, 1962). The development of characterization is a major theme of K. Reinhardt's *Sophocles.*

3. The relevant fragments are Bacchylides 64 *dub.* Snell-Maehler and Archilochus 286 West. A good survey of the sources is J. C. Kamerbeek, *The Plays of Sophocles: The Trachiniae* (Leiden, 1970), pp. 1–7.

4. "Lycorma" is another name for the Evenus. The phrase I have rendered "divine, uncanny gift" *(daimonion teras)* is used by the chorus, *Antigone* 376, when the guard brings in Antigone; Jebb there translates "a portent sent by the gods."

5. Bacchylides' Greek does not exclude an interpretation which would have the two meet, but the grammar would be strained.

6. There is an extensive, at times far-fetched treatment of this relationship in S. Kapsomenos, *Sophokles' Trachinierinnen und ihr Vorbild* (Athens: Greek Humanistic Society, 1963), pp. 38–86.

7. The Telegony, like *Women of Trachis,* ended with a son's marriage to his dead father's mistress (Allen p. 109; Evelyn-White p. 531). Parallels with the *Odyssey* are discussed by C. Segal, *Tragedy and Civilization* (Cambridge, Mass., 1981), pp. 82–83.

8. Winnington-Ingram, *Sophocles: an Interpretation,* pp. 332–33, makes a gallant attempt at reconstructing a coherent story. Possibly the text is corrupt. U. Parlavantza-Friedrich, *Täuschungsszenen in den Tragödien*

des Sophokles (Berlin, 1969), p. 27, suggests that the confused syntax represents Lichas's embarrassment—the muddle is a "psychology of the lie."

9. Deianeira, asking the chorus for silence, uses an ambiguous phrase: "You will never fall into shame, even if you act shamefully, as long as it is secret" or "even if your experience is shameful." It is thus not certain that she admits that the use of the potion is wrong, but her use of an expression which could mean this to express her embarrassment reveals her moral discomfort.

10. See C. H. Whitman, *Sophocles: a Study of Heroic Humanism* (Cambridge, Mass., 1951), pp. 104 ff., and S. Lawrence, "The Dramatic Epistemology of Sophocles' *Trachiniae*," *Phoenix* 32 (1978):288–304.

11. See chapt. 2, n. 13.

12. The disease imagery is discussed by P. Biggs, "The Disease Theme in Sophocles' *Ajax, Philoctetes,* and *Trachiniae*," *Classical Philology* 61 (1966):223. On the sexual associations of heat, see Segal, *Tragedy and Civilization*, pp. 73–75. (These are, of course, not the only patterns of imagery running through the play.)

13. A good treatment of this controversial part of the play is P. Easterling, "The End of the *Trachiniae*," *Illinois Classical Studies* 6, no. 2 (1981):56–74.

Chapter Four

1. A crucial word in this line (99) and in the drama, *philos*, means both "friend" and "relative," can be a noun or an adjective, and can be active or passive—"dear" or "loving": Ismene's words can describe Antigone's love for her relatives or theirs for Antigone.

2. Again an important line (370) is ambiguous. *Hypsipolis* can mean either "high in the city" or "having a high city"; while *apolis*, "cityless," could refer either to the exile or to one whose city is destroyed. The unusual symmetry of the poem emphasizes these words; the same assonance-in-antithesis appears in the metrically corresponding point in the preceding stanza (*pantoporos*, "all-contriving," and *aporos* "without contrivance").

3. On pollution, *miasma*, see E. R. Dodds, *The Greeks and the Irrational* (Berkeley: University of California Press, 1951), pp. 35–40; W. K. C. Guthrie, *The Greeks and their Gods* (Boston: Beacon, 1950), pp. 189–93.

4. The Cleopatra myth is obscure in its details (Sophocles may well have handled this myth himself in one of his two plays entitled *Phineus* or in *Tympanistae*), and the sequence of thought in this ode is difficult. Contrast Winnington-Ingram, *Sophocles: an Interpretation*, pp. 98–109 (the ode prepares for the explosive irrationality and violence of the play's end)

with R. W. B. Burton, *The Chorus in Sophocles' Tragedies* (Oxford, 1980), pp. 126–32 (ode merely gives examples of the power of fate over those of noble birth).

5. D. M. MacDowell, *The Law in Classical Athens* (London: Thames and Hudson, 1978), pp. 175–78.

6. *Odyssey*, 3. 255–61.

7. There is a good introduction to the "unwritten laws" in Guthrie, *The Sophists*, pp. 117–30; see also Ehrenberg, *Sophocles and Pericles*, pp. 22–50.

8. *Memorabilia*, 4. 4. 19–25.

9. The ode depends on sophistic speculation; see again Guthrie, *The Sophists*, pp. 60–83.

10. There is controversy over whether Antigone's harshness is assumed in order to save her sister (S. Adams, *Sophocles the Playwright* [Toronto, 1957], p. 51), or is rejecting her completely (J. H. Kells, "Problems of Interpretation in the *Antigone*," *Bulletin of the Institute for Classical Studies* (University of London) 10 [1963]:47–64. I do not think pretence should be read into her earlier lines or sarcasm into her later ones.

11. Line 572 is given to Ismene by the manuscripts, but these have little authority on the identity of speakers. The formal conventions of *stichomythia* (single-line exchanges) favor Ismene. But the exchange "Dearest Haemon, how your father dishonors you," with Creon's "You and your marriage are an excessive annoyance," better fits Antigone. With Jebb I would give her the line.

12. The Greek here is very difficult; some read *kopis* ("cleaver") for *konis* ("dust"). The idea of an inner Fury (a goddess of vengeance) is very bold.

13. Sophocles does not allude to the myth of Pelops's curse against Laius, who had raped his son Chrysippus.

14. That the burial is doubled purely for dramatic effect is the argument of T. von Wilamowitz-Moellendorff, *Die dramatische Technik des Sophokles* (Berlin, 1917), pp. 29–35; that the gods perform the first burial is best argued by M. McCall, "Divine and Human Action in Sophocles: the Double Burial," *Yale Classical Studies* 22 (1972):103–17. Close to my view is H. D. F. Kitto, *Form and Meaning in Drama* (New York, 1956), pp. 153–58.

15. Vigorous and completely naturalizing (but not fully convincing) explanation in A. T. von S. Bradshaw, "The Watchman Scenes in the *Antigone*," *Classical Quarterly* 12 (1962):200–211.

Chapter Five

1. It is generally agreed that *Oedipus* falls between the early group (*Ajax, Antigone*) and the late plays (*Electra* and after). Closer dating depends

on whether the plague recalls that of 429. In the entry-song, the plague is identified with Ares, who is not elsewhere a plague-god; this could reflect the war-and-plague of 429. So B. M. W. Knox, "The Date of the *Oedipus Tyrannus* of Sophocles," *Word and Action*, pp. 112–24. On the other hand, the main features of the plague are traditional, and Ares, as a god important at Thebes and hated by the other gods, may indirectly symbolize Oedipus.

2. B. M. W. Knox, "Sophocles, *Oedipus Tyrannus* 446: Exit Oedipus?" *Greek, Roman, and Byzantine Studies* 21 (1980):321–22 has reargued the case for Oedipus's exit before the prophet's final words.

3. Epic fragments: *Oedipodeia* 1 and 2, *Thebais* 1 and 2 Allen, pp. 482–87 Evelyn-White. An extensive study of the varying mythology of this family is C. Robert, *Oedipus* (Berlin: Weidmann, 1915).

4. Aeschylus frs. 169–83 Mette, 88 Smyth.

5. Aristotle, *Poetics,* 1452a 24.

6. There is an interesting discussion of how this technique inverts cause and effect in J. Culler, *The Pursuit of Signs* (Ithaca: Cornell University Press, 1981), pp. 172–76.

7. Even specialists have ignored the conventionality of this recital. Stories in tragedy tend to be told from the beginning, even though all the characters know the basic facts.

8. The importance of the riddle has been exaggerated in some interpretations (if it were vital to the play's meaning, one would expect it to be quoted); for its implications see Segal, *Tragedy and Civilization*, pp. 207, 215, 243–44.

9. That both *Oedipus* and *Antigone* criticize Periclean rationality is the thesis of Ehrenberg's *Sophocles and Pericles* (he avoids overprecise identifications of characters and real people); for Oedipus as Athens itself, see B. M. W. Knox, *Oedipus at Thebes* (New Haven, 1957), pp. 53–106.

10. E. R. Dodds, "On Misunderstanding the *Oedipus Rex,*" *Greece and Rome* 13 (1966):37–49, defines three "Heresies": that Oedipus is justly punished, that he is a puppet of fate, that the play is merely exciting melodrama. For an immense bibliography on the guilt of Oedipus, see D. Hester, "Oedipus and Jonah," *Proceedings of the Cambridge Philological Society* 23 (1977):32–61.

11. Croesus's experiment (Herodotus 1.46–49) proves that Delphi is true, but shows that all other oracles, with one possible exception, are false; Herodotus seems to see his testing of the oracle as sensible, not impious.

12. On fate and free will, the consistency of Oedipus's character, and the joint working of human and divine factors, see Knox, *Oedipus at Thebes,* pp. 33–42, and Winnington-Ingram, *Sophocles: an Interpretation,* pp. 173–78.

Chapter Six

1. In the *Odyssey,* Agamemnon's family is often cited as a point of comparison for Odysseus's (see especially 1. 35–43, 298–300; 3. 248–312; 4. 512–47; 11. 397–434). Orestes' revenge is praised, but it is not explicit that he killed his mother as well as Aegisthus, though he is said to have buried her. The matricide is explicit in Hesiod, *Ehoeae* 23a Merkelbach-West (not known to Evelyn-White). The version of Stesichorus was influential (frs. 210–19 PMG): he included Clytemnestra's dream of a serpent-son and the recognition of Orestes and Electra through a lock of hair. His version perhaps inspired the Dokimasia Painter's crater (now in Boston), showing Aegisthus killing Agamemnon (J. Boardman, *Athenian Red-Figure Vases: the Archaic Period* [New York, 1975], plate 274). The story was told in the cyclic epic *Returns* (p. 108, line 15; p. 109, line 4 Allen, pp. 254–57 Evelyn-White). Pindar tells the tale with approval of the matricide in *Pythian* 11.

2. Whitman, *Sophocles: A Study of Heroic Humanism,* p. 152, comments that "Sophocles' drama of *Electra* has always been the great enigma." It has often been thought that Sophocles ignores the problem of matricide or treats it as just because his interest is elsewhere—in depicting Electra's character, according to many critics. So U. von Wilamowitz-Moellendorff, "Die beiden Elektren," *Hermes* 18 (1883):237–38. Hence the recognition scene becomes the climax, the murders an epilogue; so K. Reinhardt, *Sophocles* (Oxford, 1979), pp. 135–61. (English translation.) If Euripides' *Electra* is considered the older, Sophocles' may be treated as a justification of Apollo (so T. B. L. Webster, *An Introduction to Sophocles* [Oxford, 1939], p. 19). On the other side, the "dark" interpretation claims that Sophocles regards the matricide as a terrible crime undertaken without Apollo's approval: so the edition of the play by J. H. Kells, and (with varying emphasis) Winnington-Ingram, *Sophocles: An Interpretation* pp. 217–41 and Segal, *Tragedy and Civilization,* pp. 249–91.

3. A good introduction to the controversy over priority in the preface of J. C. Kamerbeek's commentary on *Electra,* pp. 5–8. The fullest discussion is A. Vögler, *Vergleichende Studien sur sophokleischen und euripideischen Elektren* (Heidelberg: Winter, 1967). I myself am convinced by G. Zuntz, *The Political Plays of Euripides* (Manchester: University Press, 1955), pp. 63–70, that the earlier dating of Euripides' *Electra* is correct.

4. *Iliad,* 1. 234–44.

5. Aeschylus, *Agamemnon,* 966–67.

6. For this function of lamentation I follow W. Burkert, "Goēs: Zum griechischen 'Schamanismus,' " *Rheinisches Museum* 105 (1962):36 ff.

7. One might also think of Euripides' *Cresphontes* in which the hero claimed to be his own killer, and was almost killed by his own mother before the recognition (this lost work was produced ca. 425). Euripides'

Helen of 412 probably alludes to both *Cresphontes* and Sophocles' *Electra* when Helen suggests to Menelaus that he die "in word" and he agrees to brave the evil omen if he will profit (1051–52), but remarks "there's something old hat about this tale" (1056). False death was probably already a theatrical cliché before Sophocles' play.

8. For the spectator's forgetting that the speech is a lie, notably T. von Wilamowitz-Moellendorff, *Dramatische Technik des Sophokles* pp. 188–91; vigorous polemic against him from A. J. A. Waldock, *Sophocles the Dramatist* (Cambridge, 1951), pp. 183–84.

9. For "look to the end," note the choral tag (probably not by Sophocles) closing *Oedipus the King* (1528–30), and compare Herodotus 1. 32–33; for the metaphor of passing the post as ending life, compare *Oedipus at Colonus* 91, *Electra* 956, *Hippolytus* 87, *Children of Heracles* 1066. (I should perhaps warn the nonspecialist reader that this "metaphorical" interpretation is likely to be disputed.)

10. Close to my view of Electra's "effective language" is W. Steidle, *Studien zum antiken Drama* (Munich: Fink, 1968), pp. 91–95.

11. Euripides, *Electra,* 1105–6.

12. Although I disagree with Winnington-Ingram, *Sophocles: an Interpretation,* pp. 204–28, I am indebted to his discussion of Sophocles' Furies.

13. Contrast Aeschylus's *Agamemnon* 102–257 and the *Cypria* fragments (p. 104, lines 12–20 Allen, pp. 492–95 Evelyn-White).

Chapter Seven

1. *Little Iliad* p. 106, lines 24–31 Allen, pp. 509–11, 516–17 Evelyn-White. There are allusions to the story in Pindar (*Pythian* 1. 100–108) and Bacchylides (fr. 7 Snell-Maehler). For the lost plays our main source is the fifty-second oration of Dio Chrysostom.

2. *Iliad,* 9. 312–13.

3. Jebb's note at 626–729 argues that Neoptolemus and Philoctetes must emerge during the song, and some critics have agreed. But there is no sign of an entrance, and this strangeness is of a piece with the tone of this part of the play. T. von Wilamowitz-Moellendorff, *Die dramatische Technik des Sophokles,* pp. 278–89, aptly describes the first section of the play as a playing-out of the false situation, in which Neoptolemus's real intentions are ignored.

4. B. M. W. Knox, *The Heroic Temper* (Berkeley, 1964), pp. 123–24, calls him "a sort of spurious Achilles."

5. These lines are followed by an interpolation about Ajax, and have therefore occasionally been themselves doubted, but recent editors accept them.

6. p. 105, lines 25-106.1 Allen; p. 507 Evelyn-White.

7. Odysseus's misinterpretation of the oracle is the basis of the influential reading of C. M. Bowra, *Sophoclean Tragedy* (Oxford, 1944), pp. 261–306. A useful corrective is D. B. Robinson, "Topics in Sophocles' *Philoctetes*," *Classical Quarterly*, n.s. 19 (1969):44–51 (Greeks normally treated prophecies as allowing room to maneuver.) Also helpful is P. Easterling, "Philoctetes and Modern Criticism," *Illinois Classical Studies* 3 (1978):27–39.

8. This is very controversial. Some have thought that Odysseus must be bluffing here—but they generally assume that Odysseus is trying to save the wording of the prophecy. Favoring bluff: A. E. Hinds, "The Prophecy of Helenus in Sophocles' *Philoctetes*," *Classical Quarterly* 17 (1967):169–80. But a deception in which the audience is uninformed would not be normal technique, and although we cannot, as some have done, say that Philoctetes' lament would be ruined if we did not believe he had true grounds for it (compare *Electra*), we can note that the play seems to try to present all possible solutions to the situation, and the abandonment of Philoctetes is one of them.

9. Neoptolemus' statement at 1326 ff. resumes his words at 191–200, as well as the report of Helenus's prophecy, but the emphasis is different: the conditional part of the prophecy and its center is Philoctetes' healing, not Troy's capture. His insight is derived from his feeling and is not a matter of information.

10. A. F. Garvie, "Deceit, Violence, and Persuasion in the *Philoctetes*," *Studi classici in Onore di Quintaro Cataudella* (University of Catania, 1972), pp. 213–26, shows how the drama is structured around these alternatives.

11. See P. Rose, "Sophocles' *Philoctetes* and the Teachings of the Sophists," *Harvard Studies in Classical Philology* 80 (1976):48–105.

12. The compact is marked by Neoptolemus's physical support of Philoctetes as they prepare to exit before the epiphany; cf. O. Taplin, "Significant Actions in Sophocles' *Philoctetes*," *Greek, Roman, and Byzantine Studies* 12 (1960):25–44.

13. Some critics find the epiphany a mere concession to the facts of myth, false to the characters or a defeat for them: so I. Linforth, "Philoctetes: the Play and the Man," *University of California Publications in Classical Philology* 15, no. 3 (1956):95–156, and G. H. Gellie, *Sophocles: a Reading*, (Melbourne, 1972), pp. 156–58. Strong defense of the end in Whitman, *Sophocles: a Study of Heroic Humanism*, pp. 187–88.

Chapter Eight

1. The authenticity of the lines, however, has been doubted. In fact, it has been suggested that Sophocles invented the cult of the Semnai

at Colonus and Oedipus's place there, "transferring" all this from the Areopagus. I find this very unlikely.

2. On suppliancy, see J. Gould, "Hiketeia," *Journal of Hellenic Studies* 93 (1973):74–103; as a plot-type, R. Lattimore, *Story Patterns in Greek Tragedy* (London, 1964), 64 ff.

3. So the play can be treated as simply a patriotic piece; thus G. Ronnet, *Sophocles, poète tragique* (Paris, 1969), pp. 281–83.

4. Cf. Segal, *Tragedy and Civilization*, p. 385.

5. See Rohde, *Psyche.*

6. So most critics see the play as about Oedipus's transformation into a hero—so Bowra, *Sophoclean Tragedy*, p. 312: [Oedipus] gradually . . . feels in himself the qualities of a hero"—or his character as such, as for example I. Linforth, "Religion and Drama in 'Oedipus at Colonus,' " *University of California Publications in Classical Philology* 14, no. 4 (1951):95–192 (Linforth minimizes the religious element). That the *Colonus* is a sequel to *Oedipus the King,* showing how Oedipus is recompensed for his earlier fall, is a commonplace of criticism (B. Seidensticker, "Beziehungen zwischen den Oidipusdramen des Sophokles," *Hermes* 100 [1972]:255–73, on his first page lists expositors of this view before arguing for elaborate thematic-structural relations). But Oedipus himself comments, "It's a poor thing to raise up an old man who fell young" (595).

7. Cf. Winnington-Ingram, *Sophocles: An Interpretation,* pp. 248–79.

8. So Waldcock, *Sophocles the Dramatist,* p. 221.

Chapter Nine

1. L. Cazzaniga, *La saga di Itis nella tradizione letteraria e mitografica* (Varese: Istituto editoriale cisalpino, 1950), pp. 50–54.

2. Frs. 441-450 Radt. I depend on the discussion of W. S. Barrett in R. Carden, *The Papyrus Fragments of Sophocles* (Berlin, 1974), pp. 171–235.

3. Radt 314; translation in D. Page, *Literary Papyri: Poetry* (Cambridge, Mass.: Loeb Classical Library, 1941), pp. 26–53 (also fragments of *Scyrioi, Inachus,* and *Eurypylus*—but the papyrus once thought to be *Gathering of the Achaeans* has since been identified as Euripides' *Telephus*).

4. For the early period, see R. Pfeiffer, *A History of Classical Scholarship from the Beginnings to the End of the Hellenistic Age* (Oxford: Oxford University Press, 1968), pp. 222–23, 277; for Byzantium, L. D. Reynolds and N. G. Wilson, *Scribes and Scholars: A Guide to the Transmission of Greek and Latin Literature,* 2d ed. (Oxford: Oxford University Press, 1974), passim; for reception in the West, R. R. Bolgar, *The Classical Heritage and its Beneficiaries* (Cambridge: Cambridge University Press, 1954), pp. 504, 524–25. The latest work on the controversial history of Sophocles'

text is R. Dawe, *Studies in the Text of Sophocles,* 3 vols. (Leiden: Brill, 1973–78).

5. *Oedipus the King* has been most imitated, followed by *Antigone* and *Electra.* See J. T. Sheppard, *Aeschylus and Sophocles: their work and influence* (New York: Longmans, 1927). Interpretations of Greek tragic characters in ancient and modern dramas in K. Hamburger, *From Sophocles to Sartre* (New York: Ungar, 1969). (This was first published in German in 1962.)

6. W. McC. Stewart, "Racine's Response to the Stagecraft of Attic Tragedy as seen in his Annotations," in *Classical Drama and its Influence,* ed. M. J. Anderson (London: Methuen, 1965), pp. 175–90.

7. On German neo-Hellenism: W. Rehm, *Griechentum und Goethezeit,* 4th ed. (Bern: Francke, 1964); E. M. Butler, *The Tyranny of Greece over Germany* (Cambridge: Cambridge University Press, 1935); H. Trevelyan, *Goethe and the Greeks* (Cambridge: Cambridge University Press, 1981); F. Prader, *Schiller und Sophokles* (Zürich: Atlantis, 1954); H. Hatfield, *Aesthetic Paganism in German Literature from Winckelmann to the Death of Goethe* (Cambridge, Mass.: Harvard University Press, 1964).

8. In this section I am much indebted to R. Jenkyns, *The Victorians and Ancient Greece* (Oxford: Oxford University Press, 1980), esp. pp. 113–32, 264–74.

9. J. Gerhard, "The *Antigone* as Cultural Touchstone: Matthew Arnold, Hegel, George Eliot, Virginia Woolf, and Margaret Drabble," *PMLA* 96 (1981):22–35.

10. Among the most famous books of this group are J. E. Harrison's *Themis* (Cambridge: Cambridge University Press, 1912), and Gilbert Murray's *Five Stages of Greek Religion* (Oxford: Oxford University Press, 1925; first published as *Four Stages of Greek Religion* [1912]).

Selected Bibliography

PRIMARY SOURCES

1. Editions of Sophocles

Dain, A. French Translation by Paul Mazon. Paris: Les Belles Lettres (Budé), 1955–60. Vol. 1, *Ajax, Les Trachiniennes* (1955); vol. 2, *Antigone, Oedipe-Roi, Electre* (1958); vol. 3, *Philoctéte, Oedipe à Colone* (1960).

Dawe, R. Leipzig: Teubner, 1975–79. Vol. 1, *Ajax, Electra, Oedipus Rex;* vol. 2, *Trachiniae, Antigone, Philoctetes, Oedipus Coloneus.*

Pearson, A. C. *Sophocles Fabulae.* Oxford: Oxford University Press, 1924.

2. Fragments

Carden, R. *The Papyrus Fragments of Sophocles.* With a contribution by W. S. Barrett. Berlin: de Gruyter, 1974.

Pearson, A. C. *The Fragments of Sophocles.* 3 Vols. Cambridge: Cambridge University Press, 1917.

Radt, S. *Fragmenta Tragicorum Graecorum IV: Sophocles.* Göttingen: Vandenhoeck & Rupprecht, 1980.

3. Commentaries and Editions with Commentary

Jebb, R. C. *Sophocles: the Plays and Fragments.* Cambridge: Cambridge University Press, 1883–96. Fragments in Pearson, above. Reprint ed. Amsterdam: Hakkert, 1962; St. Clair Shores, Mich.: Scholarly Press, 1972.

Kamerbeek, J. C. Leiden: Brill, 1953–80. *Ajax* (1953); *Trachiniae* (1959); *Antigone* (1978); *Oedipus Tyrannus* (1967); *Electra* (1974); *Philoctetes* (1980).

Schneidewin, F. W., revised by Nauck. A. Berlin: Weidmann, 1910– 14. Revised by E. Bruhn: *Oedipus Tyrannus* (1910); *Electra* (1912); *Antigone* (1913). Revised by L. Radermacher: *Oedipus Coloneus* (1909); *Philoctetes* (1911); *Ajax* (1913); *Trachiniae* (1914).

4. Individual Plays

Kaibel, G. *Electra.* Leipzig: Teubner, 1896.

Kells, J. H. *Electra.* Cambridge: Cambridge University Press, 1973.

Stanford, W. B. *Ajax.* London: MacMillan, 1963.
Webster, T. B. L. *Philoctetes.* Cambridge: Cambridge University Press, 1970.

SECONDARY SOURCES

1. Bibliography
Diller, H. *Sophokles.* Darmstadt: Wissenschaftliche Buchgesellschaft (Wege der Forschung, no. 95, 1967), pp. 537–46. Bibliography for 1960–67, broken down by category but not annotated.
Johansen, H. F. "Sophocles 1939–50." *Lustrum* 7 (1962):96–342. An invaluable bibliography and discussion of work on the poet during this period (in English).
Ströhm, H. "Forschungsberichte: Sophokles." *Anzeiger für die Altertumswissenschaft* 30 (1977):129–44. Lists earlier installments of this periodic report.

2. Books on Greek tragedy
Jens, W. *Die Bauformen der griechischen Tragödie.* Munich: Fink, 1971. Essays by several authors on formal aspects of tragedy (choral entry, monody, suppliant scenes, etc.).
Jones, John. *On Aristotle and Greek Tragedy.* New York: Oxford University Press, 1962. Attacks the importation of modern notion of character and hero into Greek tragedy.
Kitto, H. D. F. *Form and Meaning in Drama.* New York: Barnes and Noble, 1956. Includes essays on *Philoctetes, Antigone,* and *Ajax.*
————. *Greek Tragedy: a Literary Study.* 3d ed. London: Methuen, 1961. Good on relation of dramatic idea to structure and on divine and human planes.
Lesky, A. *Die tragische Dichtung der Hellenen.* 3d ed. Göttingen, Vandenhoeck & Rupprecht, 1972. Sane, clear, comprehensive, and learned, with bibliographical footnotes worth hunting through even for the Germanless reader.
Pohlenz, M. *Die griechische Tragödie.* 2d ed. Göttingen: Vandenhoeck und Rupprecht, 1954. A good achievement for the approach which looks for intellectual history in signs of the poets' personal experience and opinions.
Taplin, O. *The Stagecraft of Aeschylus.* Oxford: Oxford University Press, 1977. A commentary on Aeschylus's stage technique which is enlightening also for the other tragedians.

3. Books specifically on Sophocles

Adams, S. M. *Sophocles the Playwright.* Phoenix Supplement 3. Toronto: University of Toronto Press, 1957. Despite the title, a general book, sensitive but oversimplifying.

Bowra, C. M. *Sophoclean Tragedy.* Oxford: Oxford University Press, 1944. A classic statement of the "orthodox" interpretation.

Burton, R. W. B. *The Chorus in Sophocles' Tragedies.* Oxford: Oxford University Press, 1980. A dull but useful and knowledgeable guide to the Sophoclean chorus.

Ehrenberg, V. *Sophocles and Pericles.* Oxford: Blackwell, 1954. A lively discussion of Sophocles' place in the political life of his time and of *Antigone* and *Oedipus the King* as critiques of contemporary rationalism.

Gellie, G. H. *Sophocles: a Reading.* Melbourne: Melbourne University Press, 1972. A sane, theatrically oriented treatment of the plays and major issues.

Kirkwood, G. M. *A Study of Sophoclean Drama.* Ithaca: Cornell University Press, 1958. An analysis of plot structure, characterization, and other "dramatic" questions.

Kitto, H. D. F. *Sophocles: Dramatist and Philosopher.* London: Oxford University Press, 1958. A short, informal discussion of "divine and human drama" in Sophocles.

Knox, B. M. W. *The Heroic Temper.* Berkeley: University of California Press, 1964. Lectures on the nature of the "hero," especially in *Antigone, Philoctetes,* and *Oedipus at Colonus.*

————. *Oedipus at Thebes.* New Haven: Yale University Press, 1957. A brilliant analysis of *Oedipus the King:* the hero as representative of Athens and of humanity.

Müller, G. *Sophocles: Antigone.* Heidelberg: Winter, 1967. A literary commentary which argues for constant double meanings— sometimes insightful, sometimes far-fetched.

Parlavantza-Friechrich, U. *Täuschungsszenen in den Tragödien des Sophokles.* Berlin: de Gruyter, 1969. A careful description and comparison of the scenes of deception in the extant plays.

Perrotta, G. *Sofocle.* Messina: G. Principato, 1935. Notable for chronology: Perrotta argues that in the early plays, *Antigone* and *Ajax,* the hero acts; in all the others, he only suffers.

Reinhardt, K. *Sophokles.* 3d ed. Frankfurt: Klostermann, 1947. English translation by H. and D. Harvey (Oxford: Blackwell, 1979). Studies the dynamics of Sophoclean situations: a difficult, elegant, and influential book.

Ronnet, Gilberte. *Sophocle, poete tragique.* Paris: de Broccard, 1969. Mainly on the "unhappy ending" plays; analysis of characters, sometimes excessively psychological.

Segal, C. *Tragedy and Civilization: an Interpretation of Sophocles.* Cambridge, Mass.: Harvard University Press, 1981. A structuralist treatment, which sees the tragedies as exploring cultural contradictions.

Waldock, A. J. A. *Sophocles the Dramatist.* Cambridge: Cambridge University Press, 1951. Sophocles as pure craftsman, striving solely for dramatic effect.

Webster, T. B. L. *An Introduction to Sophocles.* Oxford: Oxford University Press, 1939. "Orthodox" and rather shallow, but covers a good deal of material.

Weinstock, H. *Sophokles.* 3d ed. Wuppertal: Marees-Verlag, 1948. A philosophical meditation on Sophocles more than a close reading; very intelligent but abstract.

Whitman, C. H. *Sophocles: a Study of Heroic Humanism.* Cambridge, Mass.: Harvard University Press, 1951. A brilliant assault on the "orthodox" view of the pious Sophocles. Whitman's Sophocles is an agnostic whose heroes find divinity in themselves.

Wilamowitz-Moellendorff, T. von. *Die dramatische Technik des Sophokles.* Philologische Untersuchungen, vol. 22. Berlin: Weidmann, 1917. Argues that Sophocles sought effective scenes, not consistent characters. Extreme and sometimes insensitive, but shows that modern concern for realism should not be applied to Sophocles.

Winnington-Ingram, R. P. *Sophocles: An interpretation.* Cambridge: Cambridge University Press, 1980. Not an attempt at treating all issues, but a sensitive, individual analysis stressing the role of irrationality, echoes of Aeschylus, and the choral odes.

4. Articles

Alt, Karin. "Schicksal und *physis* im Philoktet des Sophokles." *Hermes* 89 (1961):141–74.

Benardete, Seth. "A Reading of Sophocles' *Antigone.*" *Interpretation: a Journal of Political Philosophy* 4, no. 3 (1975):148–96; 5, no. 1 (1975):1–55; no. 2 (1975):148–84.

Burian, P. "Suppliant and Savior: Oedipus at Colonus." *Phoenix* 28 (1974):408–29.

Calder, W. M. "The End of Sophocles' *Electra.*" *Greek, Roman, and Byzantine Studies* 4 (1963):213–16.

Diller, H. "Menschendarstellung und Handlungsführung bei Sophokles." *Antike und Abendland* 6 (1957):157–69.

Easterling, P. E. "Character in Sophocles." *Greece and Rome*, 2d. ser. 24 (1977):121–29.

————. "Oedipus and Polyneices." *Proceedings of the Cambridge Philological Society*, n.s. 13 (1967):1–13.

————. "The Second Stasimon of *Antigone.*" In *Dionysiaca: Nine Studies in Greek Poetry presented to Sir Denys Page*, edited by R. D. Dawe et al. Cambridge, 1978., pp. 141–58.

Erbse, H. "Neoptolemus und Philoktet bei Sophokles." *Hermes* 94 (1966):177–201.

————. "Zur Elektra des Sophokles." *Hermes* 106 (1978):284–300.

Harsh, P. W. "The Role of the Bow in the *Philoctetes* of Sophocles." *American Journal of Philology* 81 (1960):408–14.

Hester, D. A. "To Help One's Friends and Harm One's Enemies: A Study in the Oedipus at Colonus." *Antichthon* 11 (1977):22–41.

Johansen, H. F. "Die Elektra des Sophokles: Versuch einer neuen Deutung." *Classica et Medievalia* 25 (1964):8–32.

Linforth, I. M. "Antigone and Creon." *University of California Publications in Classical Philology* 15, no. 5 (1961):183–260.

————. "Electra's Day in the Tragedy of Sophocles." *U. of California Publications in Classical Philology* 19, no. 2 (1963):86–126.

Schlesinger, E. "Die Intrige im Aufbau von Sophokles' Philoktet." *Rheinisches Museum* 111 (1968):97–156.

Sheppard, J. T. "*Electra:* A Defense of Sophocles." *Classical Review* 41 (1927):2–9.

Solmsen, F. "Electra and Orestes: Three Recognitions in Greek Tragedy." *Mededlingen der koninklike Nederlandse Akademie van Wettenschappen*, Afd. Letterkunde n.s. 30, no. 2 (1967):31–62.

Torrance, R. "Sophocles: Some Bearings." *Harvard Studies in Classical Philology* 69 (1965):269–327.

Vidal-Naquet, P. "Le *Philoctete* de Sophocle et l'éphébie." In *Mythe et tragédie en Grèce ancienne*, edited by J.-P. Vernant, and P. Vidal-Naquet. Paris: Maspero, 1973, pp. 159–84.

Woodard, T. M. "*Electra* by Sophocles: the Dialectical Design." *Harvard Studies in Classical Philology* 68 (1964):163–205; 70 (1965):195–233.

Index